The Archaeology of Town Creek

T0288157

A Dan Josselyn Memorial Publication

The Archaeology
of Town Creek

EDMOND A. BOUDREAUX

THE UNIVERSITY OF ALABAMA PRESS
Tuscaloosa

Copyright © 2007
The University of Alabama Press
Tuscaloosa, Alabama 35487-0380
All rights reserved
Manufactured in the United States of America

Typeface: Minion

∞

The paper on which this book is printed meets the minimum requirements of American
National Standard for Information Sciences-Permanence of Paper for Printed Library
Materials, ANSI Z39.48-1984.

Library of Congress Cataloging-in-Publication Data

Boudreaux, Edmond A.
The archaeology of Town Creek / Edmond A. Boudreaux.
p.   cm.
Includes bibliographical references and index.
ISBN-13: 978-0-8173-1587-0 (cloth : alk. paper)
ISBN-10: 0-8173-1587-X
ISBN-13: 978-0-8173-5455-8 (pbk. : alk. paper)
ISBN-10: 0-8173-5455-7
1. Town Creek Site (N.C.) 2. Mississippian culture—North Carolina. 3. Indians of North
America—North Carolina—Antiquities. 4. Excavations (Archaeology)—North Carolina.
5. North Carolina—Antiquities. I. Title.
E78.N74B68 2007
975.6'74—dc22

2007009465

For Christy

Contents

Illustrations

FIGURES

TABLES

Acknowledgments

The efforts of many people are represented in this book, and I am grateful to them all. I want to thank everyone who has made the Town Creek site and its archaeological collection's incredible resources available for learning about Native Americans in the Southeast. Archie Smith and the staff at Town Creek Indian Mound State Historic Site have been helpful and encouraging throughout my research. Steve Davis of the Research Laboratories of Archaeology at the University of North Carolina put an incredible amount of effort into organizing the materials from Town Creek, especially the photographs and the site map. The occupational history of Town Creek could not have been investigated without Steve's previous work. I want to acknowledge the numerous field workers, lab workers, and on-site supervisors who ever worked at Town Creek or with its collections. Since 1937, much effort has gone into excavating, processing, and curating artifacts from the site. I was very fortunate to walk into a situation where I had access to an organized, well-curated collection that included tens of thousands of labeled ceramics and a number of reconstructed ceramic vessels. I also want to acknowledge Joffre L. Coe, the man who envisioned and oversaw long-term research at the site. Town Creek is an integral part of his legacy.

This book has benefited from the insights, suggestions, and ideas of many people. I want to thank Steve Davis, Kandi Hollenbach, Jon Marcoux, Mintcy Maxham, Brett Riggs, Chris Rodning, Vin Steponaitis, Trawick Ward, and Greg Wilson for the many, many ways in which they helped me during my time at the University of North Carolina (and beyond). I also want to thank the reviewers, Barry Lewis and Lynne Sullivan, and the staff of The University of Alabama Press for all their excellent suggestions. This is a greatly improved work thanks to the efforts of all these folks.

The research presented here received funding from several sources. The Center for the Study of the American South at the University of North Carolina provided a grant that partially supported the production of a geographic information systems map of Town Creek. Grants from the North Carolina Archaeological Society and the Timothy P. Mooney Fellowship of the Research Laboratories of Archaeology both went to obtaining radiocarbon dates. There are few funding sources for collections-based research in the Southeast, and I want to thank these institutions for the support they were able to provide.

My family has been there for me throughout this process. My parents, Edmond and Virginia Boudreaux, have always done whatever they could to help us along our way. My children—Anthony, Christian, and Claire Anne—have provided joy, frustration, and diversion. Finally, there is Christy. There is not much I could do without her.

The Archaeology of Town Creek

1

Mississippian Public Architecture, Leadership, and the Town Creek Community

Numerous Mississippian societies developed across the southeastern United States beginning around A.D. 1000 (Smith 1986; Steponaitis 1986). The Mississippian rubric, which covers over 800 years and virtually all of southeastern North America, encompasses a great deal of variation regarding material culture, physiography, settlement patterns, and political organization (Griffin 1967, 1985a:190; Smith 1978). Generally, Mississippian societies have been associated with relatively large populations, the increased importance of maize as a dietary staple, the construction of permanent towns and ceremonial centers, extensive trade networks, the appearance and elaboration of village-level positions of authority, and the placement of public buildings on earthen platform mounds (Griffin 1985a:63; Smith 1986:56–63; Steponaitis 1986:388–391). The appearance of Mississippian platform mounds has been taken as an indication that the communities who built them possessed certain social and political attributes that communities without mounds lacked. At the regional scale, sites with mounds generally are seen as social and political centers that integrated contemporaneous nonmound sites into settlement systems. At the community level, mounds are often seen as marking both increased vertical social differentiation and the centralization of political power (Anderson 1994:80; Hally 1999; Lewis and Stout 1998:231–232; Lindauer and Blitz 1997; Milner and Schroeder 1999:96; Muller 1997:275–276; Steponaitis 1978, 1986:389–392).

Platform mounds have been a part of Southeastern Native American communities since at least 100 B.C. (Jeffries 1994; Knight 1990; Lindauer and Blitz 1997:172). They were associated with a number of different activities and were built by societies that were economically, politically, and socially organized in very different ways (Blitz 1993a:7; Lindauer and Blitz 1997). One significant development occurred around A.D. 400, when leaders in some communities began to place their houses on top of earthen mounds—an act that has been interpreted as an attempt to legitimize personal authority by a commu-

2 / Chapter 1.

nity leader through the appropriation of a powerful, traditional, community-oriented symbol (Milanich et al. 1997:118; Steponaitis 1986:386). These early acts were followed in subsequent centuries by three major changes in political leadership that are thought to reflect the institutionalization and centralization of political power within Mississippian chiefly authority. First, while leadership positions in Woodland societies probably were attained through achievement (Steponaitis 1986:383), theoretically being open to individuals from any family, Mississippian leaders increasingly were drawn from high-ranking families in the community (Blitz 1993a:12; Knight 1990:17). Second, unlike Woodland societies in which it seems that charismatic individuals built and maintained a group of followers, Mississippian societies had offices of leadership that existed independently of any one individual (Hally 1996; Scarry 1996:4; Steponaitis 1986:983). Third, while earlier societies are thought to have made political decisions through councils in which a number of community leaders reached consensus, community-level decisions in Mississippian societies seem to have been made by a much smaller subset of community members; that is, political power became centralized (Pauketat 1994:168; Scarry 1996:11; Steponaitis 1986:388; Wesson 1998:114; but see Blitz 1993a:7 and Muller 1997:83).

It has been proposed that changes in leadership that occurred during the Mississippian period—namely, the centralization of political power—are reflected in concomitant changes in public architecture (Emerson 1997:250; Lewis and Stout 1998:231). Within the regional variant of Mississippian culture known as South Appalachian Mississippian (Ferguson 1971), platform mounds at a number of sites were preceded by a distinctive type of building called an earthlodge—a structure with earth-embanked walls and an entrance indicated by short, parallel wall trenches (Crouch 1974; Rudolph 1984). The best-known example is the building found beneath Mound D at Ocmulgee in Georgia (Fairbanks 1946; Larson 1994:108–110). It is a circular structure with a central hearth and a bench with individual seats along its wall. Based on analogy with the council houses of historic Indians (see Hudson 1976:218–226) and perhaps using the Ocmulgee structure as a prototype, earthlodges in the Southeast have been interpreted as places where a council of community leaders came together to make decisions based on consensus (Anderson 1994:120, 1999:220; DePratter 1983:207–208; Wesson 1998:109).

In contrast to the more inclusive function proposed for premound earthlodges, it has been argued that access to the buildings on top of Mississippian platform mounds was limited to a much smaller subset of the community (Anderson 1994:119; Blitz 1993a:92; Brown 1997:479; but see Blitz 1993a:184). Among historically observed Mississippian groups, mound summits contained the residences and ritual spaces of the social and political elite (i.e., chiefs and their families) (Lewis et al. 1998:17; Steponaitis 1986:390). In contrast, non-elites had limited access—both physically and visually—to mound summits (Holley 1999:30) or were excluded outright (Kenton 1927:427; McWilliams 1988:92). A compelling argument has been made that mounds were the seats and symbols of political power within Mississippian societies (Hally 1996, 1999). If this was the case and if ground-level earthlodges were more accessible than mound-summit structures, then access to leaders and leadership may have decreased over time. Thus, the sequence of change for public architecture during the Mississippian period may reflect a centralization of political power over time (Anderson 1994:119–120, 1999:220; DePratter 1983: 207–208; Rudolph 1984:40).

The idea that changes in public architecture reflect society-wide changes in relationships among individuals and groups seems plausible (see Adler and Wilshusen 1990:141; McGuire and Schiffer 1983:283). However, this relationship has not been extensively tested against the Mississippian archaeological record. While changes in public architecture have been documented at numerous Mississippian sites, our ability to explore concomitant social and political change has been hindered in many cases by the limited excavation of contemporaneous contexts within the same community. In the research presented here, some of the community-level assumptions attributed to the appearance of Mississippian mounds are tested against the archaeological record of the Town Creek site—the remains of a town located at the northeastern edge of the geographic extent of Mississippian sites (Figure 1.1). In particular, the archaeological record of Town Creek is used to test the idea that the appearance of Mississippian platform mounds was accompanied by the centralization of political authority in the hands of a powerful chief. Excavations at the Town Creek archaeological site have shown that the public architecture there follows the earthlodge-to-platform-mound sequence that is well known across the South Appalachian subarea of the Mississippian world (Coe 1995:65–82; Ward and Davis 1999:127). Work at Town Creek also has documented a majority of the site's nonmound architecture (Figure 1.2). The clear changes in public architecture coupled with the extensive exposure of the site's domestic sphere make Town Creek an excellent case study for examining the relationship among changes in public architecture and leadership within a Mississippian society.

CHIEFDOMS AND CHIEFS

It is clear from the ethnohistoric and archaeological records that chiefdom-level societies existed across the Southeast from the tenth through the eighteenth centuries (Blitz 1993a:6; Knight 1990:1; Steponaitis 1986:391). It is gen-

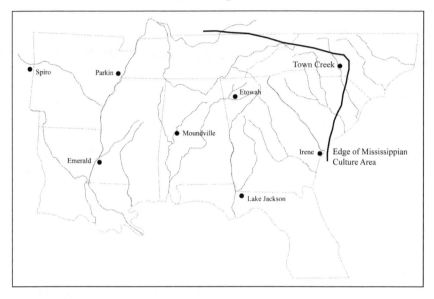

Figure 1.1. The location of Town Creek in relation to other Mississippian sites.

erally accepted that Southeastern chiefdoms consisted of multiple settlements that were integrated through shared social and political institutions (Blitz 1999:579). It is also accepted that there was an ascriptive element to the filling of leadership positions within these societies (Blitz 1999:579; Knight 1990:19). Beyond these two general points of agreement, however, there currently is a great deal of debate about the nature of Mississippian societies. The prevalent interpretation has been that the relationships among settlements within Southeastern chiefdoms were hierarchical (Anderson 1994:118; Emerson 1997; Peebles and Kus 1977:440; Smith 1978:495; Steponaitis 1978:420), but explanations that recognize the possibility that individual settlements were more autonomous have recently been offered (Blitz 1999; Maxham 2004). Chiefs in Southeastern societies have been viewed as powerful individuals with a great deal of economic and political control (Emerson 1997:249–260; Pauketat 1992:40, 1994:168; Welch 1991:180). However, alternative interpretations significantly downsize their control over people and resources (Blitz 1993a:184; Cobb 1989:89, 2000:191; Milner 1998:176; Muller 1997:56; Wilson 2001:125).

There are a number of different ways to investigate Mississippian chiefdoms. The approach that was followed when the chiefdom concept was first introduced to anthropology was one in which ethnography and ethnohistory were used to construct the attributes that constituted a model chiefdom (see

Figure 1.2. Archaeological features at Town Creek.

Carneiro 1981:38). Within this method, the documentation of one or more of these attributes archaeologically is then used to infer the presence of the others, even if these attributes are not demonstrated (see Knight 1990:2). This approach was used in some of the initial studies of chiefdoms in the Southeast (see Knight 1990:2), and it has recently been used to propose organizational variation among chiefdoms worldwide (e.g., Blanton et al. 1996). The terms "chiefdom" and "chief" will for the most part be conspicuously absent in the research presented here. These concepts are useful when clearly defined and consistently applied. Indeed, in all likelihood, the Town Creek site represents the political and ceremonial center of a simple chiefdom (see Blitz 1993a:12–

13). For this research, though, these terms are not critical and may actually be impediments because of their associated intellectual baggage. Chiefdoms, by definition, are regional entities consisting of multiple communities under the political authority of a chief (Carneiro 1981:45; Earle 1991:1). The data presented here regarding social and political change all come from a single site, Town Creek. Although it would be fascinating to explore regional-level data for the Pee Dee River Valley in the vicinity of Town Creek, such a study has not been conducted at this time. Thus, it would be misleading and of little interpretive value to talk about "the Town Creek chiefdom" when such an entity has not been defined (see Flannery 1999:45). I will instead discuss the Town Creek community. The individuals who occupied preeminent political positions at Town Creek will be referred to as community leaders, although a number of expressions would have been appropriate. The term "chief" has been avoided partly because it has come to be associated with ideas of political and economic power as well as manipulative and personally aggrandizing behavior (see Earle 1997). While these attributes and activities may have been a necessary part of political leadership in many Mississippian societies, they certainly did not exist to the same degree in them all.

THE MISSISSIPPIAN CULTURE HISTORY
OF TOWN CREEK

A South Appalachian province has been recognized as a large-scale variant within the Mississippian Southeast based on the occurrence of a predominantly complicated-stamped and non-shell-tempered ceramic tradition (Caldwell 1958:34; Ferguson 1971:7–8; Griffin 1967:190). The South Appalachian Mississippian tradition has been divided into three broad cultural units— Etowah (A.D. 1000–1200), Savannah (A.D. 1200–1350), and Lamar (A.D. 1350–1550)—that crosscut the numerous phases that constitute more localized cultural sequences (Anderson 1994; Anderson et al. 1986; Ferguson 1971; Hally 1994; Hally and Langford 1988; Hally and Rudolph 1986; King 2003; Rudolph and Hally 1985; Wauchope 1966). The spatial extent of the South Appalachian Mississippian tradition is essentially the eastern half of the Southeast, containing Georgia, South Carolina, and contiguous portions of Alabama, Florida, North Carolina, and Tennessee (Figure 1.3) (Ferguson 1971:7). The co-occurrence at Town Creek of a predominantly complicated-stamped ceramic tradition and a substructural platform mound places it within the South Appalachian Mississippian tradition (see Ferguson 1971:261).

The South Appalachian Mississippian construct contains a great deal of ceramic variation, and a number of local ceramic series and sequences have been defined within this broader tradition (Hally 1994:Figure 14.1; Williams

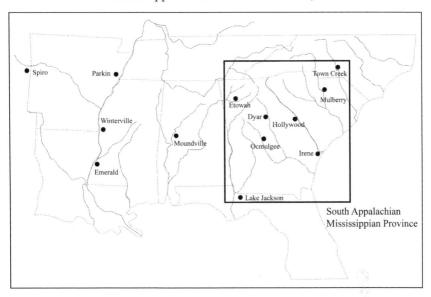

Figure 1.3. The spatial extent of the South Appalachian Mississippian tradition (based on Ferguson 1971:Map 1).

and Shapiro 1990:30–77). The Pee Dee series, which includes the Mississippian pottery found at Town Creek and surrounding sites, is one of these local variants. The geographic extent of Pee Dee culture, indicated by sites with a predominance of pottery from the Pee Dee series, as it is currently understood includes portions of south-central North Carolina and northeastern South Carolina (Figure 1.4) (Anderson 1982:313; Cable; DePratter and Judge 1990:56–58; Judge 2003; Kelly 1974; Mountjoy 1989; Oliver 1992; South 2002; Stuart 1975; Trinkley 1980). The development of the Pee Dee concept, both as an archaeological culture and a ceramic series, has been closely tied to the work of Joffre Coe. Coe (1952:308–309) gave the first definition of the Pee Dee focus based on his excavations at Town Creek, and he included a brief discussion of the Pee Dee pottery series in his landmark publication *Formative Cultures of the Carolina Piedmont* (Coe 1964:33). Later, J. Jefferson Reid, one of his students, produced the first detailed description of Pee Dee pottery from Town Creek (Reid 1967).

The Town Creek ceramic chronology fits comfortably within the South Appalachian Mississippian ceramic tradition (see Ferguson 1971). There are surface treatments and rim modes in the Town Creek–area assemblages that allow us to relate this area—under the rubrics of Etowah, Savannah, and Lamar cultures—to numerous other Mississippian sites located in the eastern

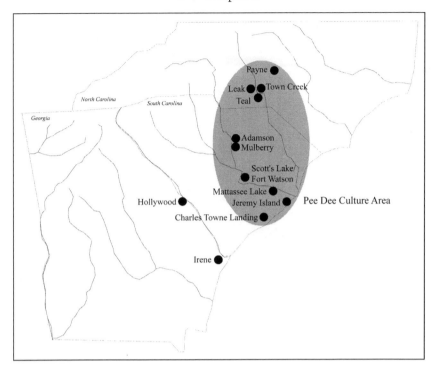

Figure 1.4. Pee Dee culture and related sites.

part of the Southeast. Oliver (1992) proposed a sequence of phases—Teal, Town Creek, and Leak—for the Mississippian period in the vicinity of Town Creek based on his excavations at the Leak and Teal sites. The ceramic content of these phases has been refined based on seriations of 11 assemblages from the Leak, Payne, Teal, and Town Creek sites (Boudreaux 2005:55–59). The temporal spans of the Teal, Town Creek, and Leak phases as presented by Oliver also have been modified based on a consideration of 15 calibrated (see Stuiver et al. 2005) and uncalibrated radiocarbon dates (Boudreaux 2005:75–80) from these four sites (Table 1.1) (Eastman 1994; Mountjoy 1989; Oliver 1992; Reid 1967).

While Town Creek ceramics are similar to South Appalachian Mississippian assemblages found to the south and west, the distinctions between Town Creek pottery and what is found to the north and east are striking. Detailed chronologies developed for the central and northern Piedmont in North Carolina (Ward and Davis 1993, 1999) indicate that these areas, located less than 200 miles from Town Creek, exhibit very different yet contemporaneous ceramic traditions that lack the distinctive rim treatments and complicated

Table 1.1. Calibrated and uncalibrated dates (A.D.) for
Mississippian phases in the Town Creek area

Phase	Calibrated	Uncalibrated
Leak	1300–1500	1300–1550
Late	1400–1550	1450–1550
Early	1300–1400	1300–1450
Town Creek	1150–1300	1050–1300
Late	1250–1300	1250–1300
Early	1150–1250	1050–1250
Teal	1000–1150	900–1050

stamping found at Town Creek. The ceramic traditions in the Sandhills and
Coastal regions of North Carolina to the east are equally distinct from that
found at Town Creek (Ward and Davis 1999). The systematic survey of nearly
100,000 acres of the Fort Bragg military reservation, located approximately
40 miles east of Town Creek, has produced only a handful of complicated-
stamped pottery (Joseph Herbert, personal communication 2005; Irwin et al.
1999:82). As Coe (1952) emphasized in his first publication on Pee Dee culture, Town Creek is clearly distinctive in the North Carolina Piedmont, and it
is one of the northeasternmost Mississippian sites in the Southeast.

PREVIOUS RESEARCH AT TOWN CREEK

Town Creek is located in the southern Piedmont of North Carolina, opposite
a bend of the Little River near the town of Mt. Gilead in Montgomery County
(Figure 1.5). It has figured prominently in North Carolina archaeology since
the late 1930s. According to Ward and Davis (1999:131): "The Town Creek
site, like a powerful magnet, has drawn the attention of archaeologists for over
sixty years. With only mild hyperbole, it could be said that the mound on the
banks of the Little River has been the center of the archaeological universe
in the southern North Carolina Piedmont."

Fieldwork began at Town Creek in 1937 and continued intermittently un-
til 1983 (Griffin 1985b:297). In 1937, Coe, then an undergraduate at UNC,
stopped taking classes in order to direct the first excavations at Town Creek
(Ward and Davis 1999:122). The site was then called the Frutchey Mound,
after the landowner who had recently donated the mound and some adjoining land to the state (Coe 1995:12). The excavation project was approved to
use Works Progress Administration labor (see Coe 1940), but eligible indi-

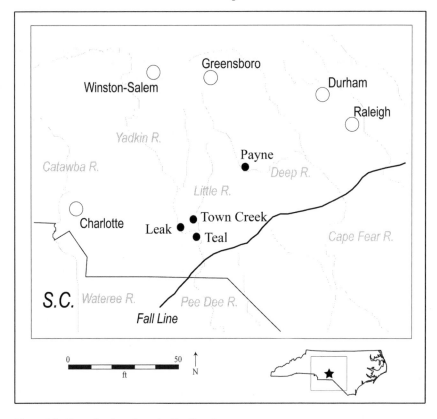

Figure 1.5. Town Creek and nearby Pee Dee sites.

viduals not assigned to other projects were scarce in Montgomery County (Coe 1995:14). Thus, the crew sizes at Town Creek were relatively small, unlike many other depression-era excavation projects that received labor from federal relief programs (see Ferguson 1995:xiii; Lyon 1996).

As was the practice at the time, the mound area (Mg^02) was given a different site number than the remainder of the site (Mg^v3) when fieldwork began in 1937. The first field seasons at Town Creek concentrated on the mound and the area immediately surrounding it. In 1937, the mound was about 12 ft high, measuring about 100 ft north-south and 90 ft east-west. Although the core of the mound was relatively intact, relic collectors in the late 1920s had severely damaged its eastern part (Figure 1.6). One looting episode included the use of mules and a drag pan to remove the eastern portion of the mound down to subsoil (Coe 1995:8). Much of the 1937 field season was spent cleaning up this earlier damage and recording the stratigraphy of the exposed face of the mound (Coe 1995:15). Most of the mound was excavated prior to 1940.

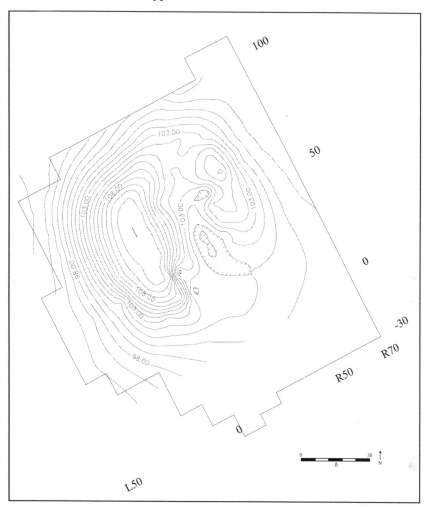

Figure 1.6. Topographic map of the Town Creek mound based on Coe's 1937 data.

The only exception was a 40-x-70-ft block near the center of the mound that was preserved.

Over 800 units measuring 10 x 10 ft were excavated in nonmound contexts at Town Creek. While thousands of nonmound features were excavated, a number of units were backfilled after they had been photographed and subsoil features were not excavated. The purpose of this was to document the location of archaeological features at the site while preserving them for future research (Ferguson 1995:xvi). Approximately 44 percent of the excavation units at Town Creek still contain five or more unexcavated features. Thus, large portions of the site were not excavated beyond the base of the plowzone, and thousands of known archaeological features are preserved at the site. According to Reid (1985:25), Town Creek "exists today as an ideal laboratory for exploring a variety of research questions."

The first description of Town Creek and its material culture was presented by Coe in his contribution to the 1952 volume *Archeology of Eastern United States* edited by James B. Griffin. In his chapter, Coe used the materials from Town Creek to define the Pee Dee focus. The interpretation that he offered then was that Town Creek represented a village occupied by a group of people who had moved into the area from the south during the mid-sixteenth century. Pee Dee culture was so different from the others that had been identified in the area that Coe was convinced it represented the movement of people from the coast into the North Carolina Piedmont and the subsequent displacement of indigenous groups. According to Coe (1952:308): "One of the best archeological records of the movement of a people in the southeast is that of the Pee Dee Culture. It moved into the upper Pee Dee River Valley with household and baggage about the middle of the Sixteenth Century, forcing the Uwharrie descendants into the hills of the Piedmont."

The next works to focus on Town Creek and Pee Dee culture were by two of Coe's graduate students at UNC. The first was J. Jefferson Reid's 1967 thesis, which presented an analysis of the pottery from the mound at Town Creek. Reid provided a detailed description of Pee Dee pottery and documented differences in the assemblages from superimposed strata. He also discussed several radiocarbon dates associated with submound and mound-summit contexts. In this thesis and in a published article, Reid (1965, 1967) noted the similarities among the pottery assemblages from Town Creek and the Irene and Hollywood sites along the Savannah River in Georgia. Based on these similarities, Reid (1967:65) proposed that these sites had been related prehistorically through an interaction sphere that he called the Town Creek–Irene axis. Billy Oliver's 1992 dissertation was on the Leak and Teal sites, two Pee Dee sites located near Town Creek. He documented his excavations at Leak and Teal and presented a number of radiocarbon dates from the sites. He also established a chronological sequence consisting of three phases for Pee Dee culture in the Town Creek vicinity (Oliver 1992:240–253).

The culmination of Coe's work at Town Creek was his 1995 book *Town Creek Indian Mound*. This volume presents a detailed account of the site's modern history, emphasizing the processes and people that have shaped archaeological research there. Here, the site was seen as being primarily ceremonial in nature with a small resident population (see also Oliver 1992:60). It was interpreted as the place where surrounding communities brought some of their dead to be buried, and the circular structures at the site were interpreted as mortuary buildings used for this purpose (Coe 1995:265–268; Oliver 1992:250). As was the case in his earlier work, Coe still saw Town Creek as the product of a group intrusive to the Piedmont, and the Pee Dee occupation of Town Creek was seen as having been relatively short in duration (Coe 1995:89–90; Oliver 1992:240).

PRESENT RESEARCH OBJECTIVES

In this book, the archaeological record of Town Creek will be used to test the idea that social and political changes accompanied changes in public architecture. One question that has guided this research has been, Did the appearance of a platform mound at Town Creek signify the centralization of chiefly political authority? This is an important question to address because it is frequently assumed that the presence of mounds in a Mississippian community indicates the presence of asymmetrical social and political relationships both within and among communities (Anderson 1994:80; Hally 1999; Lewis and Stout 1998:231–232; Lindauer and Blitz 1997; Milner and Schroeder 1999:96; Muller 1997:275–276; Steponaitis 1978, 1986:389–392). Town Creek provides an appropriate opportunity to test the potential association between the appearance of mounds and changes in political authority. The changes in Mississippian public architecture at this site, the replacement of an earthlodge with a platform mound, follow a sequence repeated at numerous sites, and this sequence has been interpreted as reflecting an increase in chiefly political authority through the replacement of a public building where councils met with a public building that was a chiefly residence.

Examining the relationship between changes in Mississippian public architecture and political changes at Town Creek provides the opportunity to delve into the extraordinary dataset that has accumulated from excavations that began in 1937. Fieldwork at Town Creek resulted in the almost complete excavation of the platform mound and the exposure of virtually an entire Mississippian town, including the extensive sampling of mound, plaza, and habitation areas. The research presented here uses architectural, mortuary, and ceramic data to explore the relationship between the evolution of public architecture and possible concomitant changes in political leadership. In Chapter 2, Town Creek's architectural features are presented in detail so that discrete units such as buildings, palisades, and mound-construction stages can be identified and dated. Architectural attributes such as shape, size, and the distribution of internal features are used to define six types of structure. Ceramic associations, radiocarbon dates, and stratigraphic relationships are used to assign structures, mound-construction stages, and other architectural units to different phases.

Dated architectural elements are used in Chapter 3 to develop a phase-by-phase history of the late Prehistoric through Historic community at Town Creek. Architectural attributes are used to make a basic functional distinction between public and domestic contexts. The evidence indicates that the Mississippian occupants of Town Creek established public and domestic contexts early in the town's history and that these areas were maintained throughout its occupation. The architectural evidence is consistent with there being no change in the form, and presumably the function, of mound-area public buildings from premound to postmound contexts. Architectural changes in the domestic sphere of the site, however, suggest that the areas north and south of the plaza shifted from residential areas early in the Mississippian period to a use as cemeteries and the location of gatherings of large groups late in the period.

In Chapters 4 and 5, mortuary and ceramic data are organized along the temporal and functional units identified in earlier chapters. The mortuary data indicate that there were changes in who leaders were and how the status of leader was expressed following mound construction. The vessel analysis suggests that the mound was not used as a residence but was used for gatherings of large groups—neither of which is consistent with a more exclusive association between a more powerful chief and the mound summit as a seat of community political authority. Architectural, mortuary, and ceramic data from Town Creek as well as regional observations are brought together in Chapter 6 to present an interpretation of how the Mississippian community at Town Creek changed throughout its history. The picture that emerges through these data is one in which changes occurred in public architecture, the use of domestic space, and the nature of leadership positions during the Mississippian period. Ceramics from the mound and consistencies in mound-area public architecture indicate that these changes, however interesting and significant, do not necessarily indicate that political power also became more centralized.

2

Architectural Analysis

The goal of this book is to explore the relationship between mound construction and political change at Town Creek. The critical first step toward reaching this goal is attributing contexts such as buildings, features, burials, mound-construction stages, and nonbuilding architecture to different time periods in Town Creek's history. Defining the spaces that served as the loci of activities in the past and contrasting the materials they contained will allow not only the recognition of activities from different periods but also contemporaneous activities—in an archaeological sense—within the same community. In this chapter, architectural elements at Town Creek are identified and dated. The spatial units and temporal relationships established here will become the basis for exploring synchronic variation and diachronic change at Town Creek in subsequent chapters.

The Town Creek site consists of a relatively clear central plaza surrounded by a dense concentration of tens of thousands of archaeological features (Boudreaux 2005). A multistage platform mound with buildings on at least two summits is located on the western side of the plaza. The dense concentration of features in submound deposits indicates that the western part of the site was intensively used prior to mound construction. For decades, archaeologists have been aware of the daunting task of sorting out the morass of postholes, pits, and burials at Town Creek, and several researchers have attempted to identify architectural patterns at the site (Boudreaux 2005; Coe 1995; Dickens 1968; South 1957b). While these efforts successfully identified buildings in some areas, it has only been since the development of geographic information systems (GIS) software that architectural elements have been systematically identified across the entire site (Boudreaux 2005; Boudreaux and Davis 2002).

Four classes of architectural elements—structures, burial clusters, palisades, and enclosures—have been identified within the postholes, pits, and burials at Town Creek (Figure 2.1). At least 42 whole or partial structures have been identified (Figure 2.2). Burial clusters are spatially discrete con-

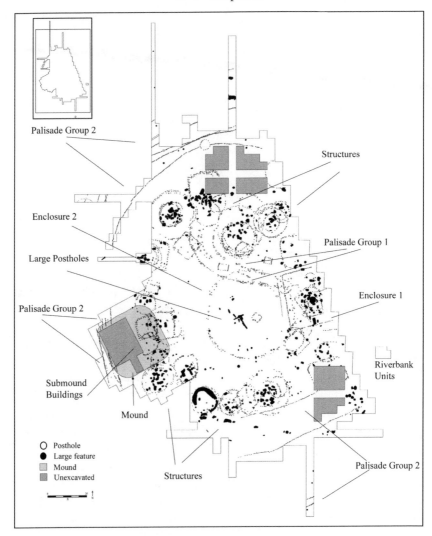

Figure 2.1. Identified architectural elements at Town Creek.

centrations of burials that could not be associated with any structure. Palisades were constructions that encircled the entire community, while enclosures were those that delineated a part of the community (see Lewis et al. 1998:18–19).

While a great deal of variation is represented in the architecture at Town Creek, several structure types have been identified based on the attributes of size and shape as well as the distribution and density of internal features. In

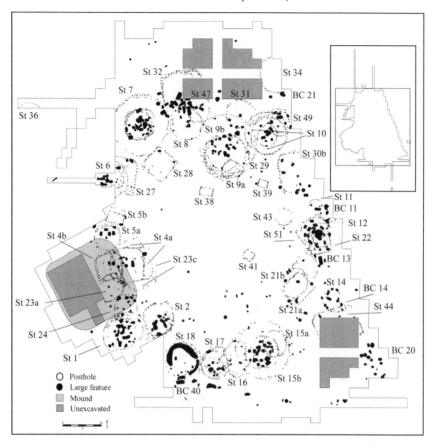

Figure 2.2. Identified structures and burial clusters at Town Creek.

this chapter, structure types will be defined, and their spatial and temporal distribution will be discussed. After a section on structure types that largely focuses on the areas north and south of the plaza where virtually all of the buildings have been assigned to a structure type, the architecture found in three other portions of the site—the mound area, the eastern area next to the Little River, and the plaza—will be presented separately because most of the buildings and architectural elements that they contain are unique and cannot be assigned to a structure type.

STRUCTURE TYPES

The most basic architectural distinction that can be made at Town Creek is between circular and rectilinear (i.e., rectangular and square) structures.

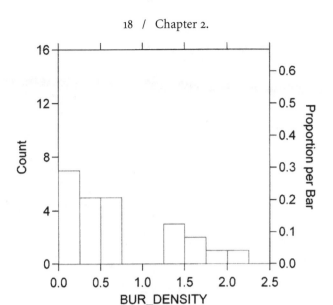

Figure 2.3. Histogram of burial density (count/100 ft²) by structure.

There is a general distinction between circular and rectilinear structures regarding the distribution and density of internal burials. Circular structures often contain dense, central clusters of burials, while rectangular ones have either fewer, scattered burials or no burials at all. Burial density is one clear distinction between circular and rectilinear structures. A histogram shows a break in the distribution of all structures by burial density (Figure 2.3). With one exception, all rectilinear structures are included in the group with burial densities less than 1 burial per 100 ft². Based on these clear differences in shape and burial density, it is useful to discuss circular and rectilinear structures separately. Even within these broad categories, enough patterned variation exists so that different types of circular and rectilinear structures can be identified.

Circular Structures

At least two different types of circular structures are present at Town Creek. One consists of a single circular pattern of posts approximately 30 ft in diameter. The other type consists of two concentric circular arrangements of posts that are approximately 30 ft and 60 ft in diameter. One possible interpretation of the two concentric patterns is that the outer circle represents the wall of the structure and the inner the remains of an interior roof support system. Alternatively, the inner patterns may represent the structure's wall while the outer pattern is an unroofed enclosure. It seems that the structure-and-enclosure scenario is more plausible for several reasons. One is that the largest exterior circular patterns, measuring about 60 ft in diameter, would have represented enormous buildings. Buildings of this size and larger have been excavated in the Southeast (Schroedl 1986:234; Shapiro and McEwan 1992:67), so they were clearly within the realm of possibility for aboriginal construction technology. However, they are usually singular examples of public architecture (see Schroedl 1986:219), referred to as townhouses, at late Prehistoric and post-Contact period sites. Not only are the Town Creek examples earlier, but if they all were roofed buildings, Town Creek would have had at least four of these distinctive structures. Another reason to think that the exterior patterns do not represent the walls of roofed structures is that the inner patterns are poor candidates for roof supports. The postholes in the inner circular patterns at Town Creek are comparable to those of the outer patterns regarding their spacing and diameters. In contrast, the postholes at Town Creek that clearly held interior roof supports—all of which are found within rectilinear structures—consist of a few large, deep, widely spaced postholes. In addition, the patterns of interior support posts within large, circular structures excavated elsewhere in the Southeast are marked by regular spacing and massive size (Schroedl 1986:Figure 4.1; Shapiro and McEwan 1992:35).

A histogram of the area of all circular posthole patterns supports the idea that the exterior patterns in concentric sets are something distinctive (Figure 2.4). There is a break in the distribution at 1,020 ft^2. All of the exterior patterns are in the group that is larger than 1,020 ft^2. Thus, there seem to be two different types of circular construction at Town Creek based on size. One type is the Small Circular Structure, which measures between about 500 and 1,000 ft^2, and the other is the Enclosed Circular Structure, which consists of two concentric circles with the outermost greater than 1,020 ft^2.

Excavated examples of Enclosed Circular Structures include Structures 1 and 7 (Figure 2.5). The interiors of these buildings contain large clusters of burials. Clear examples of unexcavated or partially excavated Enclosed Circular Structures include Structures 10 and 15b. These two buildings contain a number of large unexcavated features that are likely burials.

Small Circular Structures measure between 25 and 34 ft in diameter and do not appear to have had interior roof supports. They were likely flexed-pole constructions, consisting of posts that were individually set into the ground at one end while the other ends were lashed together to form a roof (Lacquement 2004:23; Lewis and Lewis 1995:60). These structures may have been similar to the circular flexed-pole houses built by the Caddo of the trans-Mississippi Southeast (see Swanton 1996:148–154). The interiors of excavated Small Circular Structures at Town Creek contain clusters of features, most of which

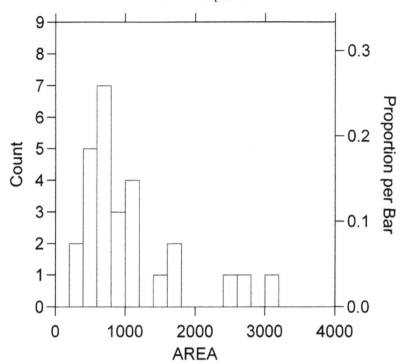

Figure 2.4. Histogram of area (ft²) of all circular structures.

were burials. Excavated examples of the Small Circular type are Structures 2, 5a, 12, 14, and 49 (Figure 2.6). In each of these cases, burials were placed in a square or circular arrangement around a central open space. Unexcavated examples of Small Circular Structures include Structures 8, 15a, 17, 31, and possibly 47, although none of these appears to have the same arrangement of internal features as the excavated Small Circular Structures. Structures 6 and 36 were only partially exposed, but their projected floor areas would place them within the range of Small Circular Structures.

A histogram of the number of burials associated with circular structures shows a break in the distribution around 20 individuals (Figure 2.7). Circular structures with fewer than 20 burials are all Small Circular, while those with more than 20 are Enclosed Circular. This distinction in the number of burials and the architectural distinction of having a large, exterior, circular pattern is consistent with Small Circular and Enclosed Circular representing two types of construction at Town Creek.

It is unclear with Enclosed Circular Structures if the structure and enclosure were standing at the same time and would be considered a single architectural element or if one was built after the other. It seems likely that Enclosed

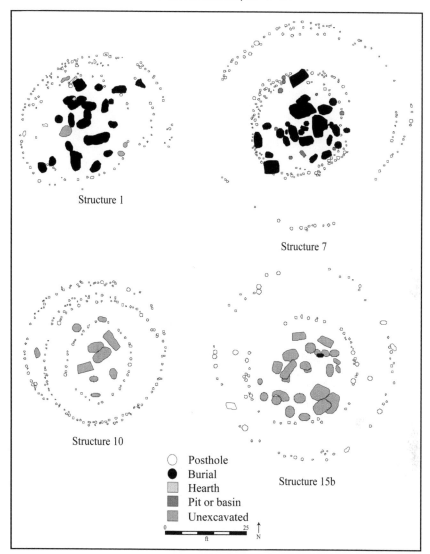

Structure 1

Structure 7

Structure 10

Posthole
Burial
Hearth
Pit or basin
Unexcavated

Structure 15b

0   25
        ft   N

Figure 2.5. Enclosed Circular Structures.

Circular Structures 7 and 15 consisted of at least a partially contemporaneous structure and enclosure because the former is centered within and seemingly constructed in reference to the latter. In the case of Structure 1, however, the inner circular pattern is not centered within the exterior pattern. In this case, it seems that the exterior pattern enclosed the structure's space but that a standing structure may not have been referenced.

Small Circular Structures represent the earliest recognized Mississippian

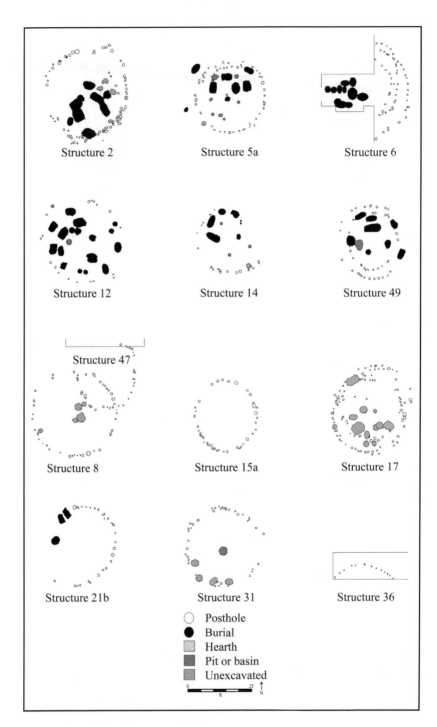

Structure 2

Structure 5a

Structure 6

Structure 12

Structure 14

Structure 49

Structure 47

Structure 8

Structure 15a

Structure 17

Structure 21b

Structure 31

Structure 36

○ Posthole
● Burial
Hearth
Pit or basin
Unexcavated

0   25
        ft   N

Figure 2.6. Small Circular Structures.

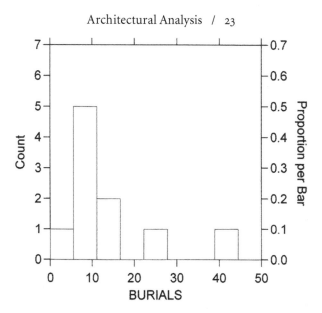

Figure 2.7. Histogram of the number of burials in circular structures.

buildings at Town Creek. The diagnostic pottery associated with Small Circular Structures is largely consistent with an early or late Town Creek phase designation (Boudreaux 2005:222). One Small Circular Structure is superimposed by the mound, and another is the earliest building in the sequence of superimposed structures in the eastern part of the site. The Small Circular Structure beneath the mound was associated with a radiocarbon date of A.D. 1010+40 (cal. A.D. 1033–1153), suggesting it was used during the early Town Creek or Teal phases (Boudreaux 2005:219). Another Small Circular Structure had a large early Town Creek phase pit located at its center. Enclosed Circular Structures appear to postdate Small Circular Structures, as the former are generally associated with pottery from the Leak phase (Boudreaux 2005:222).

Rectilinear Structures

Large Rectangular Structures are defined as those that had floor areas greater than 1,000 ft^2 and a relatively low density of interior features. The low density of features was clear in Structures 27 and 30b, both of which were largely excavated and overlapped little with other structures (Figure 2.8). Although poorly defined, structures 32 and 44 are probably Large Rectangular Structures as well. Large Rectangular Structures date to the late Town Creek or early Leak phase or later (Boudreaux 2005:222).

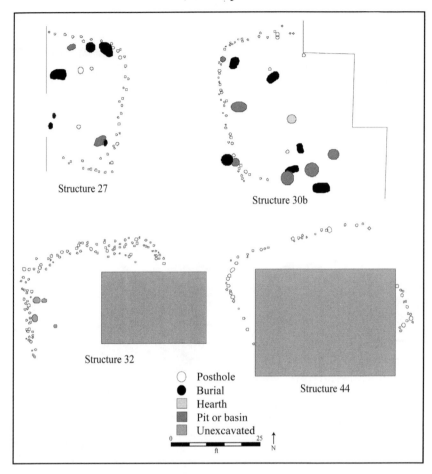

Figure 2.8. Large Rectangular Structures.

Rectilinear structures that exhibit earth-embanked walls represent another structure type at Town Creek (Figure 2.9). While a partially preserved earth-embanked wall was directly observed in Structure 23a, earth-embanked walls are inferred in the case of Structure 4b, based on the field descriptions and photographs that indicate a mass of differently colored soil around and over the structure. The probability of earth-embanked walls is also inferred for Structures 22, 45a, and 46a based on the presence of entrance trenches (see Hally 1994:154). Earth-embanked structures had four large interior roof supports arranged in a square. Nearly all of these structures had a large hearth within the area defined by the roof supports. The one exception was Structure 22, the only earth-embanked structure that had been plowed. At least

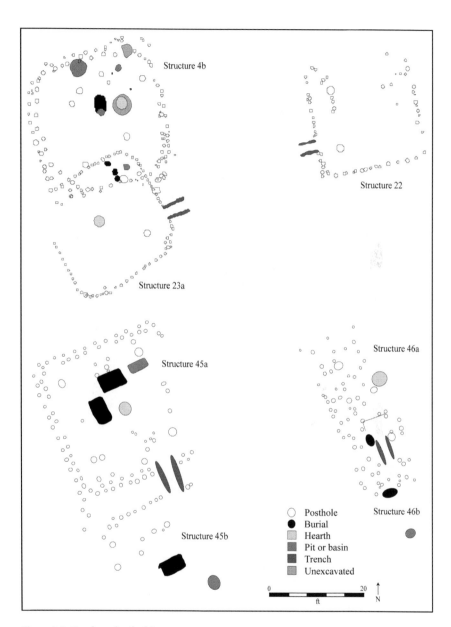

Figure 2.9. Earth-embanked Structures.

three of the earth-embanked structures were paired with other structures. It is clear from the stratigraphic sequence of submound and mound contexts that earth-embanked structures span the period that immediately predates mound construction and extends through the use of the first few mound stages (see the following section on the Mound Area). The ground-level earth-embanked structures date to the early Town Creek phase, while those on the mound summit date to the Leak phase (Boudreaux 2005:222).

Medium Rectangular Structures are almost square in appearance, and their corners are oriented to the cardinal directions (Figure 2.10). Interior roof supports are represented by four deep pits arranged in a square. There are relatively few features inside Medium Rectangular Structures, and those that are present are widely dispersed across the interior. Structure 28 is the only Medium Rectangular Structure that was fully excavated. Its interior contained four deep postholes and burials located in its northwest and northeast corners. Unexcavated examples of this type include Structures 16 and 21a, each of which had large features located in their northern corners. Structure 9a may represent the northwest corner of a Medium Rectangular Structure based on its orientation, but this structure is poorly defined at this time. Medium Rectangular Structures date to the Leak phase or later (Boudreaux 2005:223).

Four very small (< 145 ft^2) rectangular buildings have been classified as Small Rectangular Structures (Figure 2.11). Structures 38, 39, and 41 were not clearly associated with any internal features. Structure 5b was not associated with internal features either, but two burials appear to have been aligned with its walls. Small Rectangular Structures appear to date to the Leak phase or later (Boudreaux 2005:223).

MOUND AREA

The Mound Area is the western part of Town Creek that was encompassed by the Mg2 grid (Figure 2.12). Coe (1995:65–84) and Reid (1985:25–26) have discussed the sequence of events represented in the submound and mound deposits of the Mound Area. The interpretations presented in this section are based partially on their accounts but also on the photographs, drawings, and notes produced by the excavators at Town Creek.

Ground-Level Structures

The area underneath the mound was intensively used, and the result is a complex arrangement of overlapping features and structures. At least nine structures are present at ground level in the Mound Area, seven of which were wholly or partially superimposed by the mound. Four Mound Area struc-

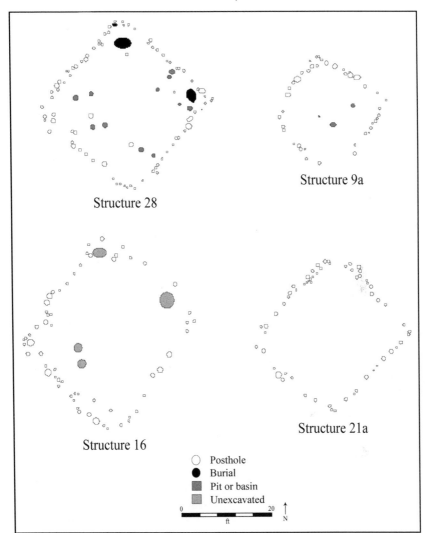

Structure 28

Structure 9a

Structure 16

Structure 21a

○ Posthole
● Burial
▨ Pit or basin
▨ Unexcavated

0   20
ft   N

Figure 2.10. Medium Rectangular Structures.

tures (Structures 1, 2, 5a, and 5b) have been assigned to structure types. The remaining five structures are unique and will be discussed in this section.

Structure 24 is a square construction that measures approximately 23 ft on a side. It contained two hearths near its center and four burials. A line of three burials was located along the structure's north wall, and a possible fourth burial was located on its south wall. This possible burial is a pit that

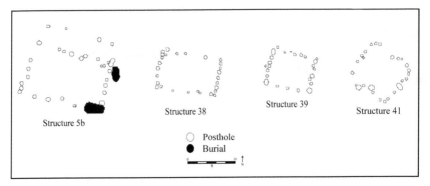

Figure 2.11. Small Rectangular Structures.

contained mostly trash but also a few human bones. Structure 24 dates to the early Town Creek phase or earlier (Boudreaux 2005:157).

Structure 4a is a nearly square structure (33 x 34 ft) that appears to have had a portico on its eastern side adjacent to the plaza. Its interior contained a number of postholes. Most of these postholes were less than one foot in depth, but four deep postholes arranged in a square appear to represent interior roof supports. This pattern of many shallow postholes and a few deep ones is consistent with the idea of having a few interior support posts surrounded by benches and other furniture (see Lewis and Lewis 1995:62). Two large hearths were located near the center of Structure 4a within the area delineated by the support posts. Two extended burials, one of an adult female and one of a child, oriented parallel to the structure, were also located within this area. A line drawn through the two extended burials and the two hearths would bisect Structure 4a along its east-west axis. This structure was superimposed by the mound, indicating that it dates to the early Town Creek phase or earlier. In addition, a corncob from a hearth within Structure 4a produced a radiocarbon date of A.D. 1130 ± 40 (cal. A.D. 1187–1261) (Boudreaux 2005:157).

Structure 4b is a nearly square building (26 x 27 ft) that appears to have rounded corners. The field notes and the excavation photographs indicate that it had earth-embanked walls. The photographs show a wide area of light soil surrounding the structure around its exterior. This area of discoloration is symmetrical, and its shape parallels that of the postholes that compose the walls of Structure 4b. In addition, the fieldnotes refer to this area of lighter soil as the structure's "yellowish streaked outer shell," and the structure itself is described as a "stratified house like an earth mass" (Swart 1940b). The exterior wall of the structure consisted in places of two rows of postholes, all of which were over 0.5 ft deep and most of which were over 1 ft deep. It is possible that these multiple rows represent rebuilding or repair events. Alternatively, the

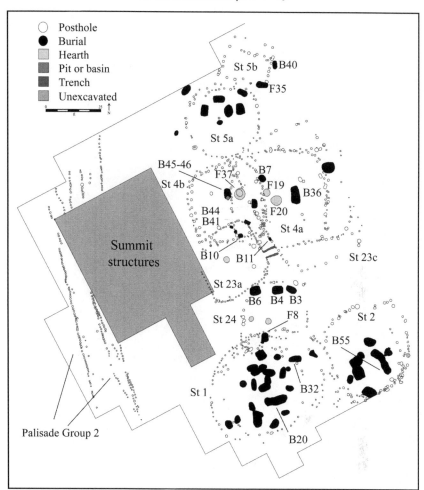

Figure 2.12. Identified architectural elements in the mound area.

depth and density of the postholes may be related to the construction needs of an earth-embanked structure. Two large, deep, interior postholes probably represent the western half of a square arrangement of roof supports. A hearth and a flexed burial were located within the roof supports. Structure 4b dates to the early Town Creek phase (Boudreaux 2005:157).

Structure 23a and Structure 23b are two rectilinear structures that were joined by an entrance trench. These buildings appear to have been the last structures in use immediately prior to mound construction, and they date to the early Town Creek phase (Boudreaux 2005:157). Structure 23a is the smaller of the two, measuring 23 ft on a side, and it is also more complete. It is

Figure 2.13. Earth-embanked wall and postholes at northeastern corner of Structure 23a, 1937: (a) moundfill (b) earth-embankment (c) Structure 23a postholes, marked by stakes, intruding a premound midden (Level A) (RLA image 191).

referred to as "the earthlodge" in publications on Town Creek (Coe 1995:65). This structure clearly had earth-embanked walls. The mound was built over the top of the structure, and the northeastern corner of its earth-embanked wall was preserved by being incorporated into the mound fill (Figure 2.13) (Coe 1995:68). This portion of the wall consisted of a 3.5 ft tall earthen embankment on the exterior of the structure packed against wall posts on the interior (Coe 1995:Figure 4.12). Structure 23a had an entrance trench, which is consistent with its walls being earth-embanked (see Hally 1994:154), near its southeastern corner on the side facing the plaza. A field map at the Research Laboratories of Archaeology (RLA) of the overall Mg2 excavations shows that the earth-embankment around Structure 23a was 4 to 6 ft wide at its base; it extended around the entire structure and tapered in thickness inward toward the end of the entrance trench (Boudreaux 2005:Figure 3.25). The interior of the structure contained four large, deeply set roof support posts arranged in a square and a large hearth within this space. A cluster of three infant burials was located in the structure's northeast corner. A fourth infant burial was located in the line of posts that compose the west wall of Structure 23c.

The entrance trenches of Structure 23a connect to the west wall of Structure 23c. Structure 23c is a very large rectangular structure, measuring 50 x 33 ft, located adjacent to the plaza. It has the same orientation as Structure 23a. With the exception of a few basins on its south end, it is difficult to associate any interior features with this structure. This is not surprising because of the complexity of the archaeological record, with at least four structures overlapping, and because this is the portion of Mg2 that would have been most disturbed by a relic collector's earlier mule-and-drag-pan excavations (see Coe 1995:8). The fact that interior support posts could not be defined for Structure 23c could mean that it did not have a roof and was more like an enclosure or that it was a lightly constructed building with a much less substantial roof than other rectilinear structures.

Mound Stratigraphic Sequence

The first mound construction at Town Creek dates to the beginning of the late Town Creek phase, approximately A.D. 1250 (Boudreaux 2005:156). Portions of the earth-embanked wall of Structure 23c were incorporated into the fill of the mound, so clearly this was the last premound structure in the Mound Area. An ash layer that contained a number of burned logs was located stratigraphically above Structure 23c and below the first mound construction stage (Swart 1940b). This ash-and-log layer covered an area approximately 60 x 30 ft with Structure 23c at its southern end (Coe 1937; Lowry 1939:5). It is unclear how far the ash layer originally extended to the north of Structure 23c. The fact that this ash layer covered a large area and that the logs were all oriented either parallel or perpendicular to each other suggests that this was not a chance burning episode. Thus, it seems that the ash layer and burned logs represent a planned event that took place prior to mound construction, perhaps the destruction of an as yet unidentified structure or some other ritual event.

The first step in the mound-building process at Town Creek seems to have been the construction of what Coe (1995:69–70) called a premound embankment (Figure 2.14) (Reid 1985:25; Swart 1940a). This embankment was made of mixed clay walls that were 3 to 4 ft tall and approximately 4 ft thick at the base (Swart 1940b). The embankment was square in shape and measured approximately 75 ft on a side. The interior of the embankment was filled with moundfill up to a level about 1 ft above the top of the embankment itself, making the first mound stage 5 ft in height. It is likely that this mound summit contained one or more public buildings, but excavations did not get down to this surface because a 40-x-70-ft block was left unexcavated near the center of the mound.

The second mound-construction stage, which dates to the early Leak phase or later, was smaller than the first, measuring only about 2 to 3 ft thick. While the first stage accounted for roughly half of the mound's final volume, the second stage constituted about a quarter of the final volume. The western edge of the summit of this second mound-construction stage contained two buildings, Structures 45a and 45b. These two structures collectively are referred to as either "Townhouse I" or "Temple I" in the field notes and draw-

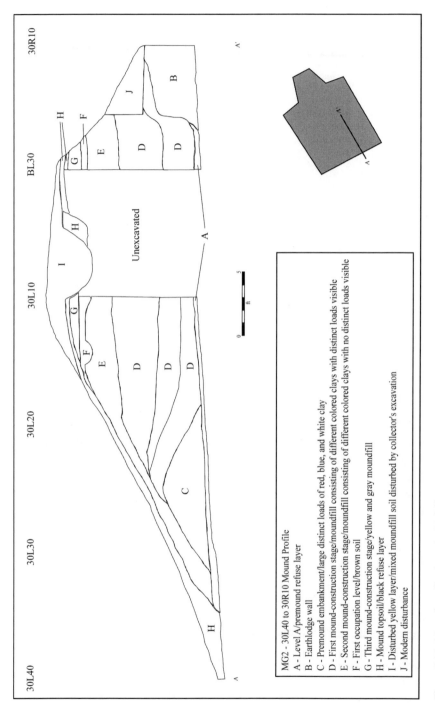

MG2 - 30L40 to 30R10 Mound Profile
A - Level A/premound refuse layer
B - Earthlodge wall
C - Premound embankment/large distinct loads of red, blue, and white clay
D - First mound-construction stage/moundfill consisting of different colored clays with distinct loads visible
E - Second mound-construction stage/moundfill consisting of different colored clays with no distinct loads visible
F - First occupation level/brown soil
G - Third mound-construction stage/yellow and gray moundfill
H - Mound topsoil/black refuse layer
I - Disturbed yellow layer/mixed moundfill soil disturbed by collector's excavation
J - Modern disturbance

Figure 2.14. Mound profile along the 30 ft line.

ings (see Coe 1995:74). Large areas of daub on the summit of the second mound-construction stage were seen as an indication that these structures had burned (Coe 1995:77). The second mound-construction stage was superimposed by a thin layer of dark soil, 3 to 6 inches thick. This layer is referred to as the "1st Habitation Level" or the "1st Occupation Level" in the drawings and field notes. It is possible that this dark soil represents a mound-summit midden associated with Structures 45a and 45b, although exactly what is represented by this layer is unclear.

The third construction stage consisted of a layer of moundfill that ranged in thickness from about 1 ft to just a few inches. Not only was the third construction stage not very thick, but, unlike previous stages, it did not cover the entire mound. This third stage was restricted to the mound summit, whereas the first and second stages had covered the sides of the mound as well. The third construction stage dates to the early Leak phase or later (Boudreaux 2005:156). The summit of the third construction stage contained two structures, 46a and 46b, arranged identically to those on the previous summit of the second mound-construction stage. These structures are referred to as "Townhouse II" or "Temple II" in the notes and drawings (see Coe 1995:74). The presence of burned wooden timbers and daub indicated that these structures had burned (Coe 1995:74).

The third mound-construction stage was covered by a dark layer, about 4 inches thick on the summit and about 1 ft thick farther downslope, that was called the Mound Topsoil by the excavators. This layer contained ceramics from the early and late Leak phase (Boudreaux 2005:156). It was covered by a layer of yellow moundfill, between 6 and 18 inches thick, that was present only on the mound's summit. This yellow layer dates to the late Leak phase or later (Boudreaux 2005:156).

Two midden layers also are part of the mound sequence. Level A was an early Town Creek phase premound midden that extended beneath most of the mound. It was located stratigraphically beneath the premound embankment and Structures 23a and 23c (Swart 1940b). Level X was a late Town Creek phase mound-flank midden on the mound's south side (Boudreaux 2005; Reid 1985:26).

Mound-Summit Structures

Any materials associated with the structures located on the eastern half of the mound, the side adjacent to the plaza, were destroyed by a mule-driven drag pan prior to the arrival of Coe in 1937. Fortunately, the excavators were able to identify structures on the portion of the mound's summit that remained. Parts of structures were identified on the summits of two construction stages dating to the early Leak phase or later. These structures were nearly identical in their layout, although they were separated by a layer of moundfill and were clearly distinct. Each summit of these two stages appears to have contained two structures connected by entrance trenches, the presence of which indicates that at least one or perhaps both structures in each pair were earth-embanked (see Hally 1994:154). The orientation of these structures parallels that of the mound. In both cases, the structure on the north side appears to be slightly smaller than the one on the south side.

On the earlier summit, the structure to the north (Structure 45a) is small and nearly square (27 x 28 ft) with slightly rounded corners (Figure 2.15). This square pattern consisted of two rows of posts. This double row of post-holes could indicate that the structure was repaired or rebuilt in place at least once, or it could be related to the construction requirements of a structure with earth-embanked walls. Four large, round features arranged in a square are likely interior roof supports. A centrally located prepared clay hearth, two flexed burials, and an empty pit were located within the area defined by the roof supports. Entrance trenches extended from this structure's south wall into a single row of posts that presumably was part of the north wall of another summit structure (Structure 45b). Only a portion of the north wall of Structure 45b and possibly part of its northwest corner were exposed. Structure 45b contained a single flexed burial and an empty pit. Both of these structures were burned.

The patterns on the later mound summit are much less clear. This summit presumably contained paired structures because its features consist of an entrance trench between two clusters of postholes (Figure 2.16). Using Structure 45a as a model, the west wall of the northern structure (Structure 46a) can be delineated. This structure contained the base of a daubed wall—which was interpreted as an internal partition (Coe 1995:74)—near the entrance trench as well as a bundle burial and a large central, prepared-clay hearth. A large deep posthole probably held the structure's northwest interior roof support. The structure to the south (Structure 46b) contained one bundle burial and a large deep pit that may have held one of its interior roof supports. Similar to the structures on the earlier mound summit, Structures 46a and 46b were burned.

The configuration of mound summit and submound buildings at Town Creek is reminiscent of the configuration documented in sixteenth-century mound-summit contexts at the Dyar site, which are attributed to the late Lamar, Dyar phase of north Georgia (Hally 1994:157; Smith 1994:34–38). The upper levels of the Dyar mound contained several construction stages and numerous structure rebuildings (Smith 1994:34–38), but there is a consistent pattern to the configuration of these sequential episodes of mound-

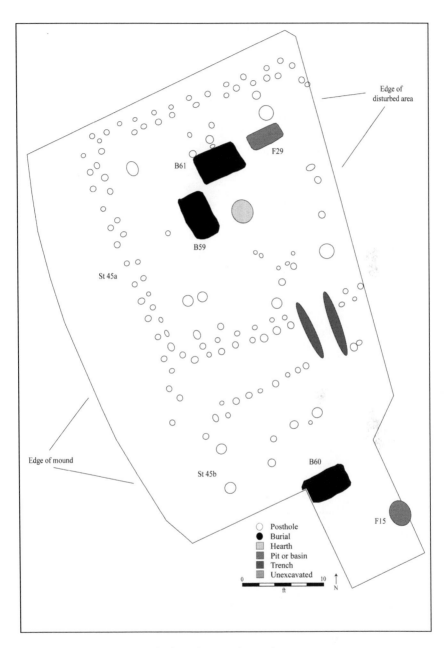

Figure 2.15. Structures 45a and 45b on the mound summit.

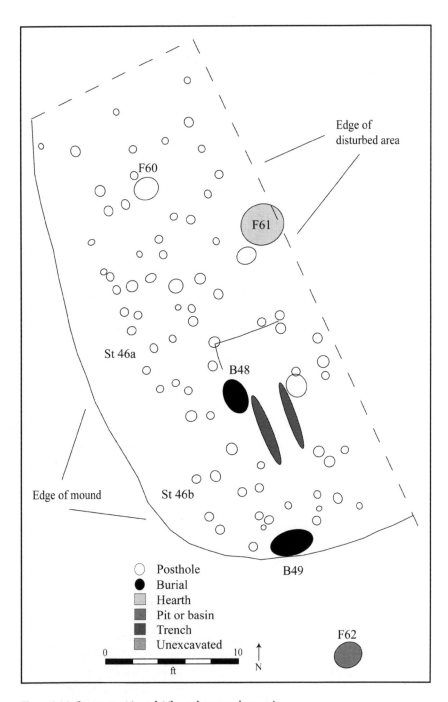

Edge of
disturbed area

F60

F61

St 46a

B48

Edge of mound

St 46b

○ Posthole
● Burial
▢ Hearth
▨ Pit or basin
▨ Trench
▨ Unexcavated

B49

0   10

ft   N

F62

Figure 2.16. Structures 46a and 46b on the mound summit.

summit architecture. This configuration consisted of two earth-embanked square structures located on the western half of the summit and one lightly constructed building that covered the entire eastern part of the summit (Hally 1994:157). Summits of the upper construction stages of the mound at Dyar consisted of two levels. Two rectangular structures possibly joined by a passageway were located on the higher western half of the mound while a larger, more ephemeral structure was located on the lower eastern half of the mound (Smith 1994:38 and Figure 14). While there were no indications of the activities that may have taken place in the northwestern structure, the presence of *Ilex* pollen in three of the structures superimposed in the southwestern part of the mound suggested to Smith (1994:38) that this may have been a place for the preparation of Black Drink, a tea that was made and consumed during the Historic period in public contexts such as council houses (Hudson 1976:372–373). The floor of the shedlike structure on the eastern part of the mound was covered with midden refuse containing sherds and animal bones. Smith (1994:38) suggests that these deposits are the remains of either domestic activities or feasting. Unlike Town Creek, no burials were found in the Dyar mound (Smith 1994:40).

The mound and submound buildings at Town Creek are also similar to those on the summit of Mound A at the Dallas phase Toqua site in eastern Tennessee (Hally 1994:157). Construction of Mound A started around A.D. 1200. A repetitive pattern of paired, substantial structures on the western half of the summit and less substantial porch or portico structures on the eastern half began with this initial summit (Polhemus 1987:1213–1214, 1990:131). This pattern of one larger structure on the eastern side and smaller structures on the western side continued for some time. Polhemus (1987:1214) interpreted the smaller structures as the dwellings of high-status individuals and the larger structures as buildings with a more public function (Polhemus 1987:1214).

Public architecture in the mound area at Town Creek always seems to have consisted of some combination of large and small rectilinear structures. At some point prior to mound construction, these public buildings consisted of a small, square, earth-embanked structure joined by an entrance trench to a large, more ephemeral, rectangular structure. This was clearly the case with Structures 23a and 23c. It is possible that the earth-embanked Structure 4b was also joined to an as yet unidentified large rectangular structure to the east. Unfortunately, there is no stage where the complete suite of public architecture for a mound summit could be documented at Town Creek. The summits of the uppermost mound stages were disturbed, the eastern half of the second and third stages was destroyed by relic collectors, and the summit of the first mound-construction stage was never reached by excavations. Thus, one can only speculate about the full complement of buildings that was located on each mound summit at Town Creek. One can make an informed guess, however, based on the premound pattern of public architecture, the portions of the summit buildings that are present, and the architectural patterns documented on mound summits at other South Appalachian Mississippian sites. It seems likely, although admittedly conjectural, that the mound-summit buildings at Town Creek were arranged as follows: on the west side were two small, square, earth-embanked structures joined by an entrance trench; on the east side was a much larger, less substantial, pavilion-like structure to which one or both of the earth-embanked structures were attached by an entrance trench.

EASTERN AREA

An enclosure (Enclosure 1), at least three overlapping structures (Structures 12, 22, and 51), and at least two burial clusters (Burial Clusters 11 and 13) were excavated in the area adjacent to the Little River on the eastern edge of the site (Figure 2.17). Structure 12, an early Town Creek phase Small Circular structure that appears to predate the other architectural elements in this area, is considered within the section on structure types and will not be discussed here.

Structure 22 was a square building measuring 21 ft on a side with an entrance trench on its west wall that faced the plaza. This structure has been referred to as the "priest's house" or the "minor temple" in the Town Creek literature (Coe 1995). Although there was no direct evidence of an earthen embankment surrounding it, the entrance trench can be used to infer the presence of such a feature at one time (see Hally 1994:154). In the case of this structure, it is likely that the remains of the embankment were obliterated by plowing (see Boudreaux 2005:178). Structure 22 dates to the Town Creek phase or earlier (Boudreaux 2005:176–178).

The interior of Structure 22 contained a square arrangement of four large, deep postholes. Lines of smaller postholes can be seen between these larger ones, indicating the presence of benches or other interior furniture. It is unclear which, if any, of the burials within the structure were actually related to it. Many of the burials in the vicinity are clearly not associated with it because they either superimpose or are superimposed by the structure. This structure 22 is very similar to Structures 4b and 23a, neither of which was clearly associated with many, if any, burials. If these two structures can be used as models, then Structure 22 may not have contained associated burials.

Structure 51 is a square construction measuring 31 ft on a side. Its orientation is about 45 degrees from that of Structure 22. It contained at least five

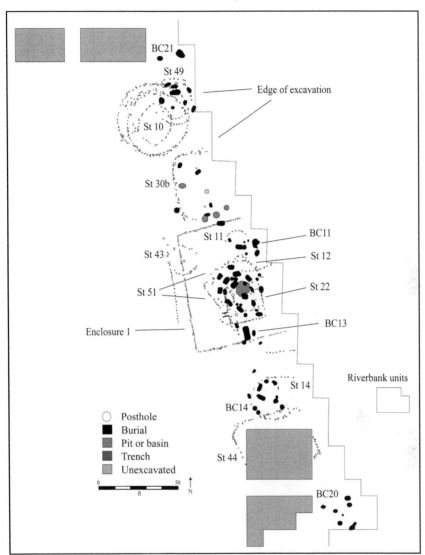

Figure 2.17. Identified architectural elements in the eastern part of the site.

burials that parallel its walls. Structure 51 has been attributed to the Leak phase (Boudreaux 2005:176–177).

Enclosure 1 is a large, rectangular construction measuring 71 x 56 ft located on the edge of the terrace adjacent to the Little River. The enclosure dates to the Leak phase or later (Boudreaux 2005:178). Only three sides of it were identified, but it is possible that the fourth was located in the adjacent unexcavated area or that it was obliterated by erosion next to the river. This construction is identified as an enclosure rather than a structure because of its large size, covering an area of at least 3,900 ft^2. Three linear arrangements of postholes—one to the west and two to the south—may be associated with Enclosure 1 and may represent rebuilding and expansion episodes of this enclosure, although complete patterns could not be identified.

Several burial clusters and at least three structures were located within the space defined by Enclosure 1. While the associations among these elements are unclear, the most obvious relationship is that Enclosure 1 and Structure 22 have parallel orientations. However, Enclosure 1 has connections with Structures 12 and 51 as well. Structure 12 is more or less centered within Enclosure 1, and Structure 51 contains a burial (Burial 20/Mg3) that is centered exactly within Enclosure 1 (Boudreaux 2005:Figure 3.46).

Enclosure 1 intrudes two burials (Burials 14 and 39/Mg3). While this is unremarkable in itself owing to the density of features at Town Creek, there are several indications that this may have been planned. First, the center of each burial is approximately the same distance, 27 and 29 ft, from the enclosure's eastern corners. Second, both individuals are oriented parallel to the line of postholes that superimposes them. Third, these two burials are aligned with the centrally located Burial 20/Mg3. Fourth, the two burials superimposed by Enclosure 1 may have been aligned with features across the plaza in the mound locus. In the earlier section on the Mound Area, it was noted that an east-west line drawn through the hearths and extended burials in Structure 4a would bisect that structure. This line also passes through a hearth, a burial, and a support post within Structure 4b. If this line was extended to the east all the way across the plaza, it would pass through Burial 39/Mg3, the burial superimposed by the southern wall of Enclosure 1 (Boudreaux 2005: Figure 3.47). Similarly, a line from the entrance trenches of Structure 23a that follows the structure's orientation, if extended to the east across the plaza, would pass through Burial 14/Mg3, the northern burial superimposed by Enclosure 1. The facts that the two burials superimposed by Enclosure 1 were the same distance from its western corners, are aligned with the centrally located burial, and may have been aligned with features of public buildings across the plaza suggest that they may have initially defined the space that was eventually delineated by Enclosure 1. This indicates that the layout of the Mississippian town at Town Creek was based on a plan that existed early in the community's history.

CENTRAL AREA

The central part of the site consists of an area with a low density of features, which is consistent with it having been a plaza (Figure 2.18). While the plaza

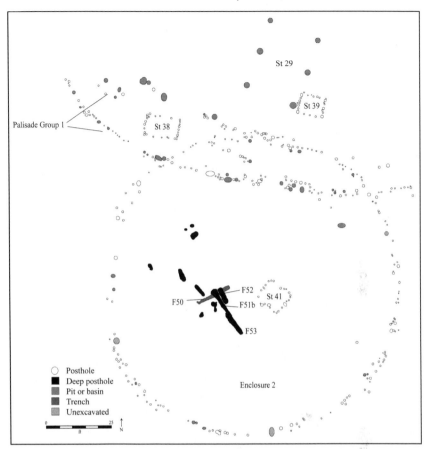

Figure 2.18. Identified architectural elements in the central part of the site.

was largely devoid of buildings, it likely was a focal point within the community (see Lewis et al. 1998:11), and it contained interesting constructions that were prominent features during the site's Mississippian occupation. Structure 41 is a small rectangular structure located in the middle of the plaza. It stands out as one of the smallest structures at the site. Eleven large, deep postholes were located in the middle of the plaza just to the west of Structure 41. Each of these postholes had a number of rocks in its fill. The postholes range in depth from 1.6 to 4.5 ft. The largest of these are three superimposed postholes between 3.6 and 4.5 ft deep that have extraction-insertion ramps extending up at a 45-degree angle from the posthole. The biggest of these, excavated and documented by Stanley South (1957a), had a 0.7-ft-deep trench perpendicular to it, the purpose of which is thought to have been to use a perpendicular log in the trench at ground level to secure and stabilize the upright pole (Coe 1995:Figure 5.8). A 2.9-ft-deep posthole with an adjacent ramp was located nearby as was a 3-ft-deep posthole that may have had an adjacent ramp. Thus, there were at least four and possibly five postholes near the center of the plaza that were around 3 ft or deeper with an adjoining extraction-insertion ramp.

Enclosure 2 is a large (112 ft in diameter) circular arrangement of posts that occupies most of the plaza. Most of this enclosure was not excavated, but the portions that were consisted of a few deep postholes (> 1 ft) and a number of shallower ones. The center of Enclosure 2 is located between Structure 41 and the cluster of deep postholes in the middle of the plaza. Enclosure 2, Structure 41, and the deep postholes may have been related and together formed a large-scale architectural unit. The eastern half of Enclosure 2 contained a number of small postholes—several of which appear to be aligned, although Structure 49 is the only clear building in the area. It may have been that, while the western half of the circular enclosure was used for the erection of large posts, the eastern half was used for the repetitive construction of small rectilinear buildings similar to Structure 49. Enclosure 2 probably predates the Leak phase (Boudreaux 2005:199).

Palisade Group 1 is a set of concentric palisade lines that runs across the Central Area and encloses the northern part of the site. Palisade Group 1 consists of up to four palisade lines, with the outermost the best defined. These palisade lines largely run through intensively occupied parts of the site, so they are not clearly defined in their entirety. Palisade Group 1 does not seem to fit within Town Creek's Mississippian site structure. It overlaps with several architectural elements, and it runs across the northern edge of the plaza. Palisade Group 1 probably predates or dates to the early end of Town Creek's intensive Mississippian occupation (Boudreaux 2005:199).

A rectangular arrangement of pits measuring approximately 20 x 30 ft has been tentatively designated as Structure 29. Although these pits are evenly spaced and approximately the same in diameter, it is not clear what they represent because other features such as walls, hearths, and burials are absent.

TOWN CREEK'S PALISADE

The entire Town Creek site was surrounded by a palisade, identified as Palisade Group 2, that was rebuilt with altered dimensions several times during the Mississippian period. Palisade Group 2 consists of at least five and possibly six concentric palisade lines that completely surround the excavated portions of Town Creek. These palisade lines were exposed in four different areas of excavation, but it is unclear how individual lines in one area relate to those in another. The concentric lines of postholes that compose Palisade Group 2 are widely spaced on the northern and southern sides of the site but are much more closely spaced in the Mound Area. This spacing is probably owing to the site's topography. The western extent of the innermost palisade of Palisade Group 2 was placed near the edge of the terrace on which the site is located, leaving little room for expansion in this direction. Palisade Group 2 does not appear to have had any bastions, although a small circular arrangement of posts associated with the innermost palisade line in the northern part of the site has been interpreted as some sort of defensive entryway (Coe 1995:87). Palisade Group 2 dates to the early Town Creek Phase and possibly later (Boudreaux 2005:153).

CONCLUSION

Long-term excavations at Town Creek have documented an extensive amount of the site's archaeological record. The extraordinary amount of architectural data from Town Creek has always been a blessing and a curse in that the excavations exposed virtually an entire Mississippian town but few discrete architectural elements could be identified, let alone dated, within the dense palimpsest of postholes, pits, and burials surrounding the plaza. Prior to the work presented here, a detailed discussion of how architecture changed through time existed only for portions of the submound and mound-summit contexts (Coe 1995; Reid 1967, 1985). This lack of spatial and temporal control has significantly hampered previous investigations of Town Creek (Anderson 1989:105; Driscoll 2001, 2002). In this chapter, arguments and evidence have been presented for the identification of dozens of structures and other architectural elements across the entire Town Creek site. In addition, associated ceramics and stratigraphic relationships have been used to date architectural elements where possible. In Chapter 3, the data presented here will be combined and elaborated upon to develop a phase-by-phase history of the Town Creek site throughout the late Prehistoric and early Historic periods. The spatial, temporal, and functional distinctions established there will then become the basis for making sitewide comparisons in subsequent chapters of architectural, mortuary, and vessel data to investigate the relationship between changes in public architecture and changes in political leadership at Town Creek.

3

Occupational History of Town Creek

This chapter presents a brief history of the late Prehistoric through early Historic period community that existed at Town Creek. Although little is known at this time about Town Creek's Late Woodland and Protohistoric occupations, information on both is included in order to place the Mississippian community within a broader context. The discussion of each phase or period consists of the buildings, burial clusters, and other architectural elements that appear to date to the same time, at least in an archaeological sense. Contemporaneity is determined directly in some cases based on associated ceramics or patterns of overlap and superposition. In other cases, it is inferred based on architectural similarities (e.g., examples of a structure type date to the same phase). Also, spatial relationships among architectural elements and overall site structure are considered.

Town Creek provides an opportunity to examine the changes that took place within a Mississippian community over a long period of time. The goal of this book is to explore changes in the nature of leadership during the Mississippian period at Town Creek, especially to contrast it in premound and postmound construction contexts. Because Mississippian leaders were strongly associated with public buildings, making a distinction between public and domestic contexts will be an important part of this discussion.

PUBLIC AND DOMESTIC ARCHITECTURE
IN THE SOUTHEAST

Mississippian towns generally can be thought of as divided into domestic and public spheres (Hally 1994:233; Holley 1999:28; Lewis et al. 1998; Polhemus 1990:134). The domestic sphere would have included the structures and facilities used and controlled by individual households to perform the production and consumption activities necessary for the household's maintenance (Wilk and Netting 1984). As the composite product of the entire community's daily activities, the domestic sphere constitutes the bulk of most archaeological collections. Assuming that domestic structures were built by household or community groups that drew from a long tradition of efficient construction techniques (see McGuire and Schiffer 1983:278), and that these techniques would have been stable and subject to only gradual change, contemporary dwellings in the same community should be similar architecturally. Since each household would have performed its activities largely independently, the domestic structures across a community should be characterized by repetitive facilities and assemblages (Winter 1976:25). In the Southeast, Mississippian houses have been identified based on their similarity in size and style as well as on the presence of artifacts and ecofacts that are consistent with domestic activities (Hally and Kelly 1998:53; Lewis and Kneberg 1970:49).

The public sphere crosscut the domestic by drawing from individual families' resources and people to fill public roles within the community (Dillehay 1990:230). The activities that took place within the public sphere included the community-level storage of resources, the performance of rituals, and the conduct of political affairs (Hally 1996:93–94). Forms of Mississippian public architecture included special-purpose buildings, delineated open spaces, monuments made from wooden poles, and earthen platform mounds (Knight 1985; Lewis et al. 1998).

Public structures, as focal points within the community, are distinct from domestic buildings for functional as well as ideological reasons (Marcus and Flannery 1996:87). Mississippian public buildings were often literally set apart, either vertically or horizontally, from the rest of the community. They were located in prominent places (e.g., mound summits, adjoining the plaza, in a central location, or on a natural elevation) (Holley 1999:30; Kelly 1990; Polhemus 1990:131; Schroedl 1998:78; Sullivan 1987:27). Mississippian public buildings often are distinguished from domestic structures by both external and internal construction characteristics. They are usually larger than contemporaneous houses (Blitz 1993a:84; Hally 1994:241; Hally and Kelly 1998:54; Holley 1999:30; Lewis and Kneberg 1970:49; Polhemus 1990:131; Rudolph 1984:33; Ryba 1997:44; Schnell et al. 1981:137; Schroedl 1998; Sullivan 1995). Unlike domestic buildings, some public structures were paired with smaller buildings (Blitz 1993a:70; Hally 1994:241; Lewis and Kneberg 1970:62; Polhemus 1990:131; Rudolph 1984:33; Schroedl 1998:70). Public buildings sometimes were oriented the same as other nondomestic buildings (Blitz 1993a:84). Some public buildings were constructed differently (e.g., with earth-embanked walls) (Rudolph 1984:33) or rebuilt more frequently (Blitz 1993a:82; Kelly 1990; Pauketat 1992:37) than domestic structures. Interiors of some public structures were distinct because of unique furniture (e.g., prepared clay altars, benches, or hearths) (Kelly 1990; Lewis and Kneberg 1970:56; Polhemus 1990:131; Rudolph 1984:33; Schroedl 1998:70), more partitions (Hally and Kelly 1998:54; Holley 1999:30; Ryba 1997:35; Schroedl 1998:70; Shapiro and McEwan 1992:10), or more open space between the central support posts (Polhemus 1990:131). In addition, many Mississippian public buildings contain burials considered to be unique because of their associated artifacts (e.g., large quantities or high quality) or age-sex composition (e.g., an overrepresentation of adult males) (Hally 1994:241–245; Polhemus 1990:131; Sullivan 1987:27, 1995:117–118).

Public and domestic structures are distinguished at Town Creek based on attributes of architecture that include size, location, and construction techniques, as well as the types and arrangements of associated features. The ensuing discussion considers the most common type of structure to be domestic, while those that have unique architectural attributes (e.g., size, pairing, placement) are considered public. Public structures are recognized using certain attributes of their construction—primarily size, orientation, and construction methods. They also are identified based on aspects of their associated burial population.

LATE WOODLAND PERIOD OCCUPATION (CA. A.D. 800 TO 1000)

Pottery that predates the Pee Dee occupation is ubiquitous at Town Creek, which clearly indicates the presence of a Woodland period occupation. Unfortunately, this component is typically manifested as a few Woodland sherds mixed with predominantly Mississippian materials (see Coe 1995:90). Structure 18 appears to be the only clearly Woodland period structure at Town Creek (Figure 3.1). It consists of a large (36 ft diameter), circular arrangement of well-spaced postholes surrounding a broad, shallow circular feature (Feature 58/Mg3). The large area encompassed by the circular posthole pattern and the lack of interior support posts is consistent with its having been an enclosure rather than a roofed building. The excavators in the field interpreted the circular feature located within this enclosure as a single large feature that superimposed and was superimposed by a number of smaller ones. Coe (1995:90) referred to this set of features as the Yadkin Hearth Circle, which was formed by "a chain of overlapping hearths contained in a circular ditch." It seems likely that Feature 58/Mg3 represents a palimpsest of numerous features—including hearths, postholes, pits, and burials—that were serially placed in the same circumscribed space. This would explain why Feature 58/Mg3 superimposed and was in turn superimposed by a number of smaller features. It would also explain why the burials within Structure 18 are all within or adjacent to Feature 58/Mg3 rather than being clustered near

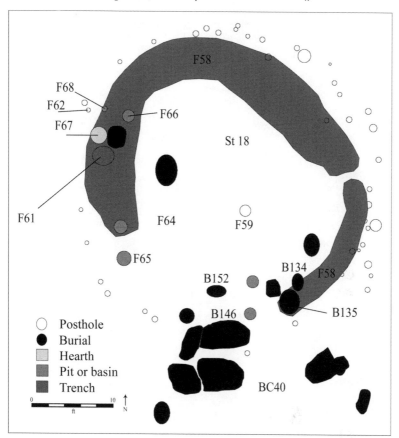

Figure 3.1. Structure 18 and Burial Cluster 40.

the building's center, as is the case with other constructions. The repetitive placement of burials and other features in a circumscribed area delineated by an enclosure is consistent with Structure 18 having been used for mortuary ritual, an important part of Woodland period societies at various times and places in the Southeast (Steponaitis 1986:379).

Structure 18 and Feature 58/Mg3 are similar to features that have been documented at several sites in western North Carolina and eastern Tennessee. One is at Coweeta Creek in western North Carolina, where a shallow, segmented, circular ditch feature with an opening to the southwest was excavated (Rodning 2004:107). According to Rodning (2004:353–354), this feature predates the Middle Qualla phase founding (A.D. 1500–1650) of the town at Coweeta Creek. The Coweeta Creek and Town Creek features are approximately the same size, with the former about 40 ft in diameter (Rodning 2004:

107) and the latter 36 ft. Interestingly, the circular ditch features at Town Creek and Coweeta Creek are also similar in that they both occupy the same location relative to each site's plaza and single mound. Both are located at the southwest corner of the plaza, just south and east of the mound (Rodning 2004:111). A similar ditch feature, which was associated with Woodland period Napier-series pottery, was excavated at the Cullowhee Valley School site in western North Carolina (Rodning 2004:353). A comparable feature also was found at the Townsend site in eastern Tennessee (Brett Riggs, personal communication 2004), where it has been interpreted as a Woodland mortuary structure.

Although Burial Cluster 40 partially superimposes it, Structure 18 was largely not superimposed to the same degree as other structures located around the plaza, even though it is the oldest identified structure at Town Creek. Based on this, it seems likely that its location was marked in some way, possibly by a low earthen mound. In southeastern North Carolina, just to the east of Town Creek in the Sandhills region and southern Coastal Plain, a sand burial mound tradition marks the Late Woodland period (A.D. 800–1000) (Irwin et al. 1999:79; Ward and Davis 1999:206–210). Most of these burial mounds are circular with a diameter between 25 and 50 ft (Ward and Davis 1999:206). Structure 18 is 36 ft in diameter, which fits comfortably within this range. There is a wide variation in the number of people interred in these mounds, from 10 to 300, and in the types of interments represented (e.g., primary and secondary) (Irwin et al. 1999:61; Ward and Davis 1999:207). The seven burials in Structure 18, all in a flexed position, approximate this range of variation. Stone pipes are frequently found with burials in these sand mounds (Irwin et al. 1999:73–78). Two stone pipes were found with a burial in Structure 18. One is a straight stone smoking tube. The other is a winged, bent-tube pipe with incised geometric designs that is similar to a pipe from the McLean mound (Irwin et al. 1999:Figure 11), a Late Woodland sand burial mound located near the Cape Fear River in Cumberland County (Ward and Davis 1999:207) that produced a radiocarbon date of A.D. 970 + 110 (Irwin et al. 1999:62).

In summary, the Late Woodland community at Town Creek appears to have consisted of a single circular structure that may have been used for mortuary rituals. This building was possibly covered by a low mound that was standing when the initial Mississippian community was founded, and it is possible that this mound was incorporated into the spatial structure of the Mississippian community. The sand burial mounds of the Coastal Plain were located away from habitation sites (Ward and Davis 1999:207) and are seen as vacant ritual centers that served dispersed populations (Irwin et al. 1999:80). The ubiquity of Woodland pottery at Town Creek but the dearth of Woodland features are consistent with the site having served initially as a vacant ritual center.

TEAL PHASE OCCUPATION (CA. A.D. 1000 TO 1150)

There are several indications that Town Creek was occupied during the Teal phase, but the evidence is not definitive. Ceramics diagnostic of the Teal phase are present, although in very small numbers. Also, there are several architectural elements (e.g., Structure 29 and Palisade Group 1) (Figure 3.2) that appear to date to the early end of Town Creek's Mississippian occupation but that do not fit within the spatial plan of the early Town Creek phase community, suggesting that they predate this phase. Based on this evidence, it is possible that a small-scale, intermittent, or as yet largely unexcavated occupation of Town Creek took place during the Teal phase.

EARLY TOWN CREEK PHASE OCCUPATION (CA. A.D. 1150 TO 1250)

The earliest identifiable, intensive occupation of Town Creek occurred during the early Town Creek phase. This occupation consists of a ring of at least 10 Small Circular Structures surrounding the plaza (Figure 3.3). It is likely that these buildings were dwellings. The clustering of burials and postholes associated with them suggests that these buildings were moved only slightly or were rebuilt in the same place during the early Town Creek phase. A gap in the western part of this ring of structures contains at least five superimposed rectilinear structures that were public buildings. The shifting and rebuilding of public structures contrasts with the fact that many Small Circular Structures were rebuilt in place. Structures 4a and 24 were the first public buildings. These were followed by the earth-embanked Structure 4b, which was likely paired with a large rectangular structure to its east. The paired Structures 23a and 23c—an earth-embanked structure and a large rectangular building that was more ephemeral in construction—were last. It is possible that Structure 22—an earth-embanked building located across the plaza—was in use at the same time as Structure 23a. The two are identical in construction, approximately the same size, and oriented the same. If they were in use at the same time, the two earth-embanked buildings would have faced each other across the plaza with the large circular enclosure between them (Figure 3.4). The entire town was surrounded by a palisade that was rebuilt several times during the early Town Creek phase.

The most obvious architectural distinction during the early Town Creek phase occupation is between circular and rectilinear structures. There are

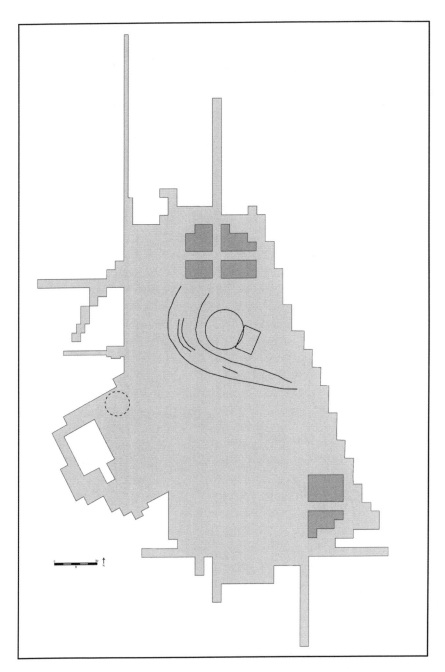

Figure 3.2. Schematic map of possible Teal-phase architectural elements (Note: dashed line indicates structure that may date to this occupation).

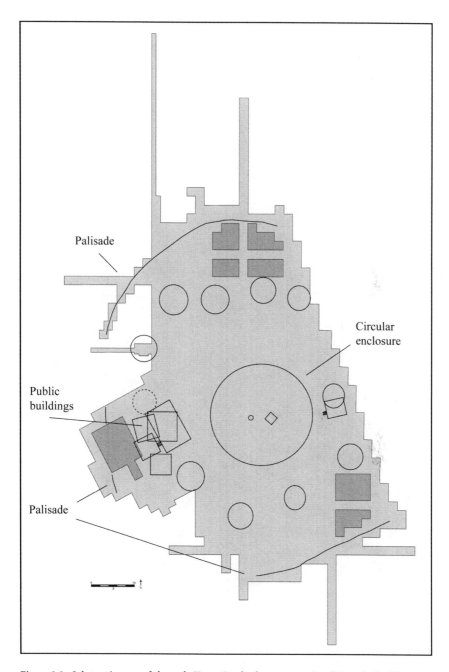

Figure 3.3. Schematic map of the early Town Creek-phase occupation (Note: dashed line indicates structure that may date to this occupation).

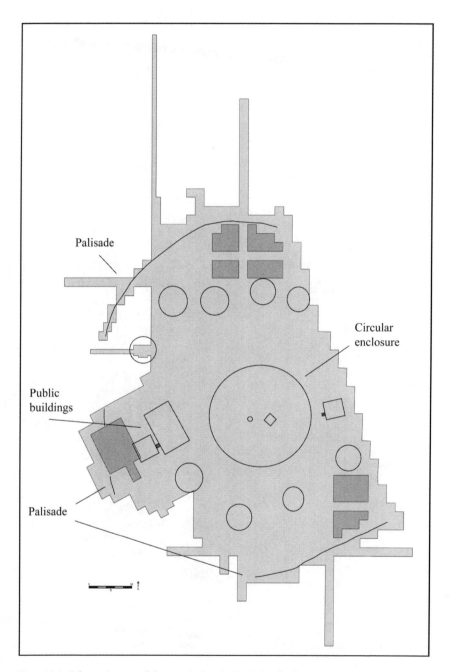

Figure 3.4. Schematic map of the terminal early Town Creek-phase occupation.

several reasons to believe that the rectilinear structures were public in nature. Circular structures are the most numerous and widely distributed, suggesting that they were dwellings. In contrast, the location of the rectilinear structures in only two parts of the site, locations that later in time would be covered by a platform mound and delineated by an enclosure, is consistent with their having been public buildings. The relatively frequent rebuilding of rectilinear structures on the west side of the plaza and their reconfiguration through time are qualities shared with public buildings at other Mississippian sites (Blitz 1993a:82; Kelly 1990; Knight 1985:113–114; Pauketat 1992:37). Also, two of the rectilinear buildings—structures 4a and 23c—during the early Town Creek phase were much larger than other buildings, a common characteristic of Mississippian public buildings (Blitz 1993a:84; Hally 1994:241; Hally and Kelly 1998:54; Holley 1999:30; Polhemus 1990:131; Rudolph 1984:33; Ryba 1997:44; Schnell et al. 1981:137; Schroedl 1998; Sullivan 1995). While the other three rectilinear structures—Structures 4b, 22, and 23a—are within the same size range as circular domestic structures, these rectilinear structures are distinct because they had earth-embanked walls and at least two of them had entrance trenches. Earth-embanking is a common feature of public buildings in the South Appalachian Mississippian area (Hally 1994:154).

The idea that circular and rectilinear structures probably functioned differently during the early Town Creek phase occupation is supported by a difference in burial density between the two (Boudreaux 2005:Figure 4.5). The distribution of structures by burial density shows a break at 1 burial per 100 ft^2 (Figure 3.5). Structures with burial densities less than this are all rectilinear and located in submound contexts while those with densities greater than this are all Small Circular Structures found across the rest of the site. The fact that posthole densities, used as a proxy measure of duration of structure use, are higher for rectilinear structures during this occupation indicates that the differences in burial density are not the result of rectilinear structures being used for a shorter amount of time than circular ones (Boudreaux 2005:243). Instead, the lower burial densities for rectilinear structures suggest that different sets of criteria determined who could be buried within each type of structure, with those criteria used for circular structures being more inclusive than those used for rectilinear ones.

There are clear relationships among all of the rectilinear structures. Structure 22 faces Structure 23a across the plaza. Structures 23a and 23c were joined by an entrance trench. Although the exact spatial and chronological relationships are unclear, internal features of Structures 4a and 4b suggest that these structures were built in reference to each other (Boudreaux 2005:126). Also, Structure 24 is located close to and oriented the same as Structure 4b. The existence of paired structures—clearly the case with Structures 23a and 23c,

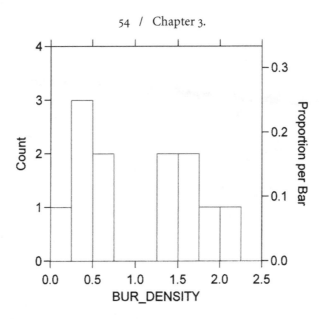

Figure 3.5. Histogram of burial density (count/100 ft²) in early Town Creek-phase structures.

possibly so with Structure 4a, and probably so with Structures 4b and 24—is a common element of Mississippian public architecture (Blitz 1993a:70; Hally 1994:241; Lewis and Kneberg 1970:62; Polhemus 1990:131; Rudolph 1984:33; Schroedl 1998:70).

The plaza was mostly open during the early Town Creek phase occupation, but it did contain a very large monument consisting of individual posts arranged in a circular pattern. One or more large posts were probably in use within the western part of the circle's interior, as indicated by deep postholes with rocks in their fill. It is possible that a series of small buildings was located in the eastern part of the interior. Instances of large, centrally located posts in native Southeastern towns are well documented both ethnohistorically and archaeologically (Anderson 1994:221; Hally and Kelly 1998:50; Knight 1985:106). Such poles may have acted as *axes mundi*—ritually defined, tangible connections between this world and other spiritual worlds (Knight 1985:107). It is plausible that the large posts in the plaza at Town Creek served similar functions. The large postholes with insertion ramps in the plaza at Town Creek are similar to large pits at several other Mississippian sites, some of which were located on mound summits (Knight 1985:106; Pauketat 1993: 31 and Figure 3.6; Ryba 1997:10–16). It is likely—based on the size of the pit and post as well as the central location of the work—that the erection and removal of these posts were prominent events within the community at Town Creek. It is possible that the largest postholes, those with extraction-insertion ramps, were correlated with mound construction episodes, as there are five such posts and at least four mound-construction stages (David Hally, personal communication 2003). The extraction-insertion ramps adjacent to several of the large postholes in the plaza are perpendicular to the site's public axis, suggesting that they were aligned with an overall site plan as well.

Enclosure 2 is at least superficially similar to the Cahokian circular monuments, which are referred to variously as woodhenges or postcircle monuments (Pauketat and Emerson 1997:14 and Figure 1.6). The Cahokia woodhenges consist of very large, regularly spaced posts of red cedar (Smith 1992:15). These monuments may have served as celestial observatories, calendrical devices, or surveying instruments (Demel and Hall 1998:216–218; Smith 1992). It is likely that one of the most critical functions that these monuments served was as world center shrines that acted "to gather and direct powers of nature and to serve as a location for communication with the forces of nature" (Hall 1996:125). If the circular enclosure at Town Creek was celestially aligned, it may have served to link the built environment of the town to the motions of the cosmos, thereby infusing the former with the power and sanctity of the latter (see Brown 1997:479).

LATE TOWN CREEK AND LEAK PHASE OCCUPATIONS (A.D. 1250 TO 1350)

The late Town Creek phase was marked by the presence of a platform mound on the western edge of the plaza, over the area that had been occupied by public buildings during the early Town Creek phase (Figure 3.6). Public buildings probably stood on the summit of the first construction stage, but excavations did not extend down to this surface. Based on the public buildings that were excavated immediately above and below and the configuration of mound summit buildings at other South Appalachian Mississippian sites (Hally 1994:157; Polhemus 1987:1213–1214, 1990:131; Smith 1994:38 and Figure 14), one can speculate that the late Town Creek phase public buildings on the mound consisted of a large, ephemeral rectangular building on the eastern side, closest to the plaza, and one or more small, square, earth-embanked buildings connected by entrance trenches on the western side, away from the plaza.

Public architecture during the early Leak phase included the addition of construction stages to the platform mound. Unlike the large construction stage of the late Town Creek phase, though, the layers added to the mound during the early Leak phase were much smaller. Portions of buildings were identified on the summits of the two mound-construction stages attributed to the early Leak phase. Unfortunately, most of these two surfaces had been destroyed when the eastern part of the mound was excavated by relic collec-

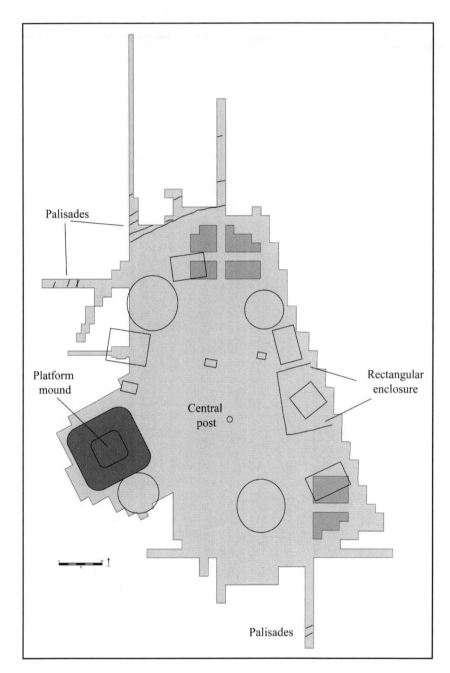

Figure 3.6. Schematic map of the late Town Creek–Leak phase occupation.

tors. The buildings that remained were located on the western edge of the mound summit, on the side of the mound away from the plaza. The architecture that was preserved consisted of two rectilinear buildings joined by an entrance trench, suggesting that they were earth-embanked, on each construction stage. The location of these buildings on a mound summit as well as the fact that they were paired and probably earth-embanked are all attributes consistent with their having been public structures (Hally 1994:154). Although there is no way to know what the building on the plaza side of the mound was like, information from other mound sites (Hally 1994:157; Polhemus 1987:1213–1214, 1990:131; Smith 1994:38 and Figure 14), as well as the configuration of submound public buildings, can be used to offer an informed speculation. It is plausible that the public buildings on the mound consisted of a large, ephemeral rectangular building on the eastern side closest to the plaza and two or more small, square earth-embanked buildings on the western side away from the plaza.

Enclosure 1 was built on the eastern side of the site at some point during the late Town Creek–Leak phase occupation. The fact that this area may have been delineated by burials aligned with features of submound public buildings indicates that a plan existed early in the site's history for incorporating the eastern edge of the plaza as a public area into the overall site structure (Boudreaux 2005:170). Although it is not clear if Structure 22 and Enclosure 1 were in use at the same time, the facts that they are located close to each other and have the same orientation indicate that they were related, even if only as diachronic forms of public architecture in the same area. Structure 51 was located within the space delineated by Enclosure 1. Structure 51 is unique because it has a very different orientation than all contemporaneous structures. Its location within an enclosure and the uniqueness of its orientation are consistent with its having been a public building. Burial clusters 11 and 13 were also located within Enclosure 1. Although the activities that took place within Enclosure 1 are unknown, it is clear that this area, presumably including some or all of the burials and structures that it contained, was set apart from the rest of the site.

The presence of the rectangular enclosure next to the river during the Leak phase means that the circular enclosure in the plaza could not have been standing at this time since the two overlap. While there is not direct evidence that the large posts near the center of the plaza were in use during the late Town Creek–Leak phases, they may date to this period because their erection may have been related to episodes of mound construction (David Hally, personal communication 2003). The three Small Rectangular Structures aligned across the north side of the plaza may date to the late Town Creek–Leak phase occupation, although they could date to a later time. The fact that they are

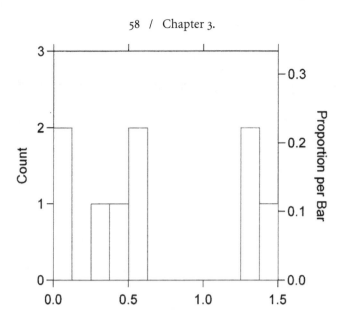

Figure 3.7. Histogram of late Town Creek–Leak phase structures by burial density (count/100 ft²).

all approximately the same size, oriented the same way, and located in a line along the north side of the plaza strongly suggests that they were contemporary and served a similar function, although it is unclear exactly what that function was. South identified one of these buildings, and it was interpreted as a shed analogous to structures used by historic Creeks during community rituals (Coe 1995:96). The location of Small Rectangular Structures within the plaza and away from the zone of superimposed structures on the plaza's periphery indicates that they may have been related more to plaza activities than to domestic ones. It seems likely that some of the outer palisade lines were also in use during the late Town Creek–early Leak phase, but there is no direct evidence for this.

The distribution of late Town Creek–Leak phase structures by burial density shows a gap at 1 burial/100 ft² (Figure 3.7), the same distinction that was noted with early Town Creek phase structures. During the late Town Creek–Leak phases, all structures with densities less than 1 burial per 100 ft² were rectilinear. Some of these were located on the mound and within the area delineated by Enclosure 1. The others were Large Rectangular Structures, which seem to alternate with Enclosed Circular Structures around the plaza. Structures with a burial density greater than 1 burial per 100 ft² include Enclosed Circular Structures and a single Small Rectangular Structure.

It is hard to identify clearly domestic architecture during the late Town Creek–Leak phases. Small Rectangular Structures are too small and there are too few of them. Large Rectangular Structures are more ubiquitous, but their size (>1000 ft^2) suggests that they were not domestic in nature. Based on the early Town Creek phase patterns, the low burial density of Large Rectangular Structures is not consistent with their having been domestic buildings.

It is unclear what is represented by Enclosed Circular Structures. The two most plausible possibilities are that they represent a contemporaneous structure and enclosure or that the pattern is a palimpsest of an earlier structure and a later enclosure. Each possibility has different implications for interpreting the late Town Creek–Leak phase occupations at Town Creek. If Enclosed Circular Structures represent a contemporaneous structure and enclosure, one could assume that, based on its size, the structure was domestic. Obviously, though, Enclosed Circular Structures cannot be viewed simply as typical houses because the presence of an enclosure signals that these were special in some way, possibly as public buildings or the residences of important people within the community (Blitz 1993a:84; DePratter 1983:118; Holley 1999:29; Larson 1971:59; Payne 1994:223).

If the enclosures and structures date to different periods, a plausible interpretation of Enclosed Circular Structures is that they represent an area recognized as a former house site that was delineated by an enclosure and used as a cemetery after the house itself was no longer in use. Within this scenario, Enclosed Circular Structures began as Small Circular Structures occupied during the early Town Creek and possibly the initial late Town Creek phases but were enclosed and used as cemeteries at some point during the latter phase. There are two cases in the eastern part of the site where structures of the Small Circular type overlap with Enclosed Circular Structures, indicating that they could not have been standing at the same time. Based on the fact that the Small Circular Structures were clearly present during the early Town Creek phase and that several lines of evidence show Small Circular Structures to be the oldest Mississippian buildings at Town Creek, it is plausible that the Small Circular Structure was occupied first, during the early Town Creek phase. The presence of late burials within Enclosed Circular Structures provides direct evidence that they were used as cemeteries in the later stages of their existence.

In summary, there is an apparent absence of domestic architecture during the late Town Creek–Leak phases at Town Creek, at least in the exposed parts of the site adjacent to the plaza. During this time, the earlier houses that had surrounded the plaza were replaced by cemeteries and large rectangular buildings. The cemeteries seem to have started as domestic structures during the early Town Creek phase and were later enclosed by a circular wall of wooden posts. The primary structure type in use at the same time as these enclosed cemeteries was a large rectangular structure with a relatively low density of interior burials.

It seems plausible that Enclosed Circular Structures began as houses—in the floors of which burials were placed—occupied by a family group. These house sites were later maintained by these groups—which may have been lineages or clans—as places where members could continue to be buried, even though people were no longer living there. Although the pattern is by no means clear, it may have been the case that Enclosed Circular and Large Rectangular Structures alternated around the plaza during the late Town Creek–Leak phases and that one of each structure type together constituted a pair of structures that was itself a functional unit. One structure in this pair appears to have served as a cemetery in which most group members were buried, while the other structure, based on its size, served as a place for the entire group to meet and as a place where a select portion of the group could be buried.

LATE LEAK PHASE OCCUPATION (CA. A.D. 1350 TO CA. 1450)

While the upper mound contexts were disturbed and no summit architecture could be identified, one can assume that a building was located on the mound summit during the late Leak phase. Based on the depth of the layers that were preserved, mound construction was minimal during this time and did not add significantly to the mound's volume. There is no direct evidence for the existence of plaza architecture or a palisade surrounding the site during the late Leak phase occupation, although there is no direct evidence that these features did not exist.

At least three Medium Rectangular Structures date to this occupation, one along the north side of the plaza and two along the south side (Figure 3.8). Two of these structures are aligned along a northeast-southwest axis on the south side of the plaza, while a third is across the plaza along a northwest-southeast axis. It seems likely that there are more structures located along these axes that are either unexposed or exposed but undefined at this time. A possible Medium Rectangular Structure on the northeastern side of the plaza may represent a fourth building that dates to this occupation.

The site structure that existed during the late Leak phase occupation was distinctive from earlier patterns. The corners of Medium Rectangular Structures are oriented to the cardinal directions, which is unusual among rectilinear structures. This orientation clearly deviates from the orientation of the mound, which still would have been the most prominent feature at the site. Also, the apparent arrangement of Medium Rectangular Structures into rows

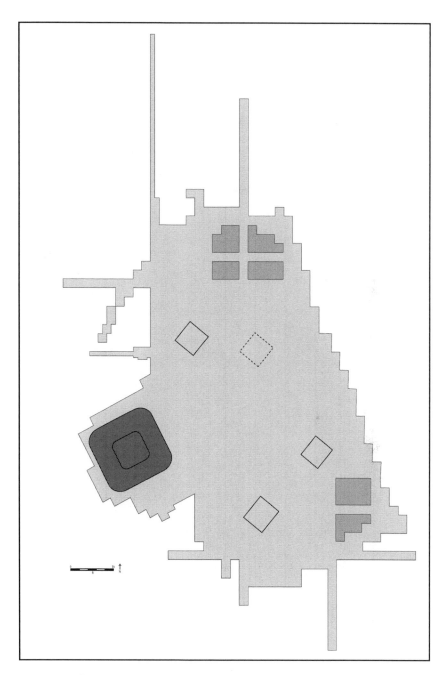

Figure 3.8. Schematic map of the late Leak phase occupation (Note: dashed line indicates possible structure).

trending southwest-northeast would have reorganized the plaza and reoriented the spatial structure of the entire site.

CARAWAY PHASE OCCUPATION
(CA. A.D. 1550 TO 1700)

Little can be said about the Protohistoric occupation of Town Creek. The presence of glass beads in the upper layers of the mound indicates that it was used during the Caraway phase (A.D. 1500–1700) (Ward and Davis 1999:134–137), although these layers were disturbed so Protohistoric activities and architecture could not be identified. Away from the mound, two Protohistoric cemeteries were located in the southeastern part of the site near the Little River (Figure 3.9). One of the Protohistoric burials contained a circular brass gorget with a small central hole, a type that postdates A.D. 1630 (Waselkov 1989:123).

Over 3,000 glass beads were recovered at Town Creek (Boudreaux 2005: Table 4.1), and their dates span the time from A.D. 1500 to 1800 (Deagan 1987: Table 4). Almost 90 percent of the beads from Town Creek came from the Mg2 area, and nearly all of these came from the upper layers of the mound. The presence of these beads is important because it indicates that the mound summit continued to be used into the Contact period. Most of the types represented were used for hundreds of years, so they tell little about a more specific period of use. The one exception is an unfaceted chevron bead from the mound, Kidd and Kidd (1970) type IVK4, which has a more specific date range of A.D. 1550 to 1650 (Deagan 1987:Table 4). The low number of glass beads away from the mound, which suggests that the beads were acquired prior to regular contact with Europeans (see Ward and Davis 1999:254), is consistent with the early seventeenth-century date suggested by the unfaceted chevron bead. Two other Piedmont phases in which European goods are present but in low numbers are Jenrette (A.D. 1600–1680) and Middle Saratown (A.D. 1620–1670) (Ward and Davis 1999:237, 247), both of which date to the seventeenth century. The absence of wire-wound beads at Town Creek is consistent with the Caraway phase occupation predating the late seventeenth or early eighteenth centuries (Brain 1979:115; Deagan 1987:175).

CONTINUITY IN SITE STRUCTURE
AND PUBLIC ARCHITECTURE

Throughout the history of Town Creek, there is an overall continuity in the use of space that implies that the residents of the community were not only aware of preceding activities and constructions but that they also acknowledged these earlier events. A large-scale example is the maintenance of the in-

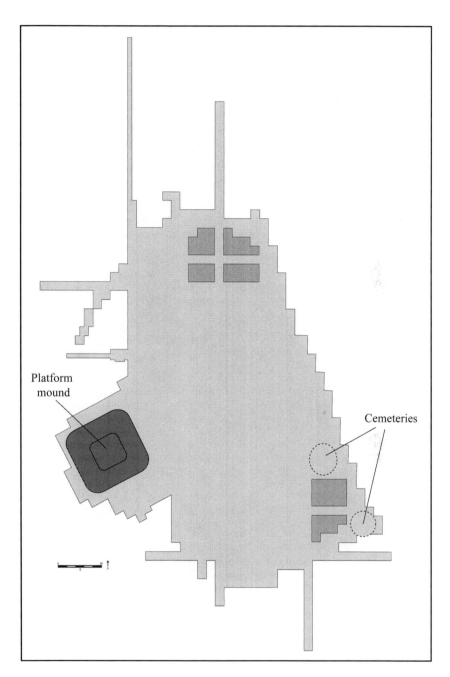

Figure 3.9. Schematic map of the Caraway phase occupation.

tegrity of the plaza by the placement of buildings on its periphery. The plaza appears to have been used for nondomestic purposes throughout the history of the site, and it contained only a few special-purpose structures. In contrast, the periphery of the plaza contained a palimpsest of structures from every stage of the community's history. Thus, it was acknowledged throughout the occupation of the site that structures were to be built in a zone surrounding the plaza while the plaza itself was to remain open. Coe (1995:265) noted that even the post–Pee Dee people respected this tradition and placed their dead around the outer limits of the plaza. Another example of continuity is that the Late Woodland mortuary structure largely was not superimposed by later structures, even though it was built early in the site's history. It is possible that this structure was marked in some way, perhaps by being covered with a low mound. Not only was this structure not superimposed, but it also seems to have been incorporated into the site structure of the subsequent Mississippian community. The overall map of Town Creek shows this structure as one of many circular structures located along the plaza.

The Enclosed Circular Structure type provides another clear example of continuity but this time within the framework of an overall functional change. These structures seem to have started as houses but evolved at some point into enclosed cemeteries. Thus, there was continuity in the occupation of a space, which may have been associated with a particular kin group, while the way in which that space was used seems to have changed significantly. The changes in the orientation of buildings and the overall site structure that occurred later during the late Leak phase occupation are striking within this overall pattern of continuity, although the maintenance of the plaza during this period represents some continuity.

Several points of continuity were present within Town Creek's public architecture. A public axis appears to have existed within the site structure of the community throughout the Mississippian period. This axis includes (1) the western part of the site, which was always used for public architecture; (2) the plaza, which included a large circular monument and massive central posts; and (3) the space defined by Enclosure 1, which included two burial clusters and at least two rectilinear structures. Another point of continuity within the public architecture is that some of the buildings beneath and on the mound appear to have been laid out in reference to earlier public buildings. In the submound contexts, the two earth-embanked structures appear to have been aligned with features of buildings that they superimposed. On the mound summit, the structures located on superimposed mound-construction stages clearly have the same floor plan. Other points of continuity within the mound-related public buildings are the presence of paired public buildings during several periods in the site's history.

CONCLUSIONS

The analysis of architectural patterns, the distribution of diagnostic ceramics, and the ranges of radiocarbon dates from Town Creek all suggest that the site was occupied for hundreds of years during the late Prehistoric and early Historic periods. Intermittent occupation began in the tenth century during the Late Woodland period and may have continued through the middle of the twelfth century at the end of the Teal phase. Intensive occupation began during the early Town Creek phase and continued for 200 to 300 years. The occupation of Town Creek became less visible and probably more episodic in nature during the fifteenth century, a pattern that continued through the seventeenth century.

The Mississippian occupation of Town Creek has been interpreted as the remains of an intrusive culture that occupied the Piedmont of North Carolina for a relatively short period of time (Coe 1952:308, 1995:89–90; Oliver 1992:240). Possible continuity between the Late Woodland and Mississippian occupations of Town Creek does not support the idea of an intrusive culture. Also, radiocarbon dates from submound contexts relate Town Creek to a growing body of evidence for the widespread presence of Early Mississippian culture—also represented at the Payne (Mountjoy 1989) and Teal (Oliver 1992) sites—in southern North Carolina. While the Mississippian culture represented at Town Creek is markedly different from the small-scale societies documented to the north and east (Ward and Davis 1999), the ceramics and site structure of Town Creek are very similar to those documented to the south and west (Anderson 1989; Cable 2000; DePratter and Judge 1990; Hally 1994; Ward and Davis 1999). It seems plausible that Town Creek's existence can be accounted for through the adoption of Mississippian ways by a local Late Woodland group rather than the migration of people into the area.

Town Creek was located on the northeastern edge of the Mississippian world. Earlier interpretations presented Town Creek as a briefly occupied frontier community that was surrounded by hostile neighbors. The occupational history presented here does not support this interpretation. During the late Prehistoric period, Town Creek was occupied at least intermittently for about 700 years. The site was intensively occupied as a formal town with a consistent site structure for between 200 and 300 years, beginning around A.D. 1150. Although located on the periphery of the Southeast, the community at Town Creek evolved and thrived for centuries, demonstrating a history whose development parallels and longevity rivals sites located nearer the core of the Mississippian world (see Anderson 1994:219; Cable 2000b).

4

Mortuary Analysis

Town Creek's rich mortuary record (Davis et al. 1996; Driscoll 2001) is a critical dataset for an exploration of the relationship between changes in Mississippian public architecture and changes in the nature of leadership. The interpretations presented in this chapter are based on the assumption that individuals who occupied leadership roles within the Mississippian community at Town Creek are recognizable within the site's mortuary record. Community leaders should be identifiable based on distinctions in where they were buried, how they were buried, and the objects that were interred with them. The community history established in Chapter 3 will be used as a diachronic framework to explore changes in who community leaders were and how roles associated with community leadership were expressed before and after mound construction at Town Creek.

A great deal of variability exists at Town Creek in the ways individuals were treated at death. The dimensions on which this variability is expressed include the position of the body within the grave (flexed or extended), evidence for postmortem processing of the body (secondary bundle burial), the location of the burial (in public or domestic contexts), and the kinds and quantities of associated artifacts. The mortuary analysis presented here is based on the assumption that the spaces in which individuals were buried, the position in which they were placed, and the items that were interred with them reflect the statuses the individuals held in life and the social roles they played within their community (see Binford 1971:13–15; Saxe 1970, 1971).

The ethnohistoric record of the Southeast supports the idea that an individual's social status had a great deal of influence on his treatment at death (Brown 1971:104–105). Ethnohistoric and ethnographic observations indicate that native Southeastern Indian communities contained individuals who fulfilled numerous social and political roles. These included various grades or types of warriors, priests, and community leaders (Hudson 1990:61–67; Lefler 1967:210; Scarry 1992; Swanton 1979:641–665; Waselkov and Braund

1995:118; Worth 1998:92). Based on cross-cultural studies (Binford 1971) and the documentary record from the Southeast in particular, social and political factors may explain much of the variation in the mortuary record at Town Creek. While the mortuary rituals of some societies actually obfuscate distinctions that existed in life, the consideration in this research of nonmortuary contexts from across the site should allow the recognition of any stark disjuncture between the daily expression of social and political differences and their manifestation in death (see Hodder 1982:152–153).

In this chapter, mortuary data are used to explore leadership roles and how they may have changed through time at Town Creek. Leadership is a status that is marked within many small-scale societies worldwide through the differential treatment of individuals at death (Feinman and Neitzel 1984:57; Flannery 1999; Marcus and Flannery 1996; Whalen and Minnis 2000:172). Artifact distributions can be useful in this regard. If objects signified a particular status held in life, then burials of community leaders—as individuals who hold the most diverse number of roles in small-scale and middle-range societies—should contain a greater diversity (i.e., high richness) of associated objects (Howell 1995:129, 1996:63; Kintigh 2000:104). Therefore, one of the ways in which Town Creek burials are compared is the number of artifact types (NAT) included as grave goods (see Bennett 1984:36; Howell 1995:129, 1996:63; Kintigh 2000:104). Also, the presence of artifacts that are distinctive within the context of a particular community (e.g., copper plates and axes, stone celts, the remains of litters, conch shells) have been recognized as symbols of particular leadership statuses in some Mississippian cases (Blitz 1993a:104; Brown 1971:101; Peebles and Kus 1977:439; Scarry 1992:179). Another way to recognize leaders is that they may be set apart physically from others, for example, being buried in special places within the community such as public spaces (DePratter 1983:189; Sullivan 1995:117). Also, the remains of leaders may have been processed in distinctive ways. The ideas of special burial location and extra processing were combined in the practice among Mississippian groups of venerating past chiefs through the storage of their cleaned and bundled skeletal remains in mound-top temples (Brown 1997:475). In addition, leaders may have been set apart by the arrangement of their bodies within the graves (e.g., orientation, seated vs. prone, extended vs. flexed, etc.) (Marcus and Flannery 1996:84–85) as well as by the form of the grave itself (Sullivan 1995:118–119).

The interpretations presented here are based partially on contrasting the individuals and artifacts associated with public buildings with those found in domestic structures. Public buildings in Historic Southeastern native towns were architecturally, socially, and politically the most prominent buildings in the community. They were the loci of daily meetings concerning intracommunity and intercommunity decision-making (Braund 1999:144; Lefler 1967:42–43; Waselkov and Braund 1995:62, 102; Worth 1998:93). They also were often the locations of important social events such as community-wide ceremonies and the entertaining and housing of significant guests (Lefler 1967:43–47; Waselkov and Braund 1995:85; Worth 1998:93). It is clear in the ethnohistoric and ethnographic records that there were social proscriptions regarding who had access to public buildings. In some cases, access was always limited to a certain social group (Kenton 1927:427; McWilliams 1988:92; Sattler 1995:220; Waselkov and Braund 1995:102, 149; Worth 1998:88). In others, access may have been more limited in some situations and more inclusive in others (Speck 1979:120). Based on the few funerals in public buildings documented in the historic record, it is clear that the person being interred in the public building in death was also one who could access the building during life (Swanton 1911:138–157). Assuming that the public buildings at Town Creek were similar to those documented in the ethnohistoric record in regard to function and social proscriptions determining access, then the activities that took place within public buildings at Town Creek probably involved primarily community-level decision-making and the hosting of intracommunity social events. If it is also assumed that the people buried in public buildings were individuals who frequented those buildings in life, then it is likely that the people buried within public buildings at Town Creek were influential in the community's political life.

The social groups responsible for the buildings and burials located to the north and south of Town Creek's public axis were likely kin-based entities such as lineages and clans. Among Historic native groups in the Southeast, regional tribal units were subdivided into a small number of clans (Knight 1990). For example, the Cherokees were divided into seven clans (Gearing 1958:1150) and the Choctaws into six to eight (Swanton 1993:79). Clan membership was matrilineal with each person becoming a member of his or her mother's clan at birth (Hudson 1976:185). Clans were manifested at the local level as matrilineages, which often consisted of a single household or group of closely related households organized around a matriarch (Hudson 1976:189; Knight 1990:6). Historic native communities were composed of multiple matrilineages that represented several different clans (Hudson 1976:190; Knight 1990:6). While clans were only weakly corporate groups, members of matrilineages met often, and it was matrilineages that controlled access to particular economic resources such as agricultural land (Hudson 1976:193; Knight 1990:5–6).

In addition to an exploration of who was buried in public and domestic spaces, mortuary data will also be used to examine relationships between gender and political leadership in the Mississippian community at Town Creek. Gender, along with kinship, was a fundamental social distinction that affected virtually every aspect of an individual's life in Southeastern Native groups (Eastman and Rodning 2001; Hudson 1976:260; Perdue 1998:8). A gendered division of labor within these groups was based upon strong social proscriptions regarding the behaviors considered appropriate for each gender group (Claassen 2001:20–25; Rodning and Eastman 2001:3; Thomas 2001:34). In general, men's activities included intercommunity activities, such as warfare and trading, and women's activities included intracommunity activities, such as food production and household responsibilities (Rodning 2001:80–82; Thomas 2001:29–34). Regarding positions of political leadership, ethnohistoric accounts indicate that men overwhelmingly occupied the role of community leader, although accounts of female chiefs are not uncommon (Sullivan 2001:102; Waselkov and Braund 1995:153; Worth 1998:88). While men are most frequently discussed as leaders in written accounts, male political power was not absolute, nor were women absent from the political process (Sullivan 2001:102). In many Southeastern communities, it is likely that men and women drew from different, complementary sources of political power and that each group served as a check on the power of the other (Perdue 1998:13; Rodning 2001:81–82; Sullivan 2001:103).

THE TOWN CREEK MORTUARY RECORD

The Town Creek burial population (Davis et al. 1996; Driscoll 2001) includes 239 individuals, of whom 218 have been attributed to Mississippian contexts, 7 from a Late Woodland structure, and 14 from two Protohistoric burial clusters (Boudreaux 2005:413–419). In this section, the Mississippian mortuary record of Town Creek is examined in regard to burial type, burial position, and demographic profiles associated with individual structures and structure types. In addition, demographic profiles, artifact distributions, and the locations of burials are used to explore the expression of community leadership roles and how these might have changed through time.

Early Town Creek Phase

The early Town Creek phase community consisted of a series of submound public buildings and an adjacent village consisting of at least 10 Small Circular Structures. In this section, the mortuary record associated with these two parts of the community is discussed. Early Town Creek phase burials largely or wholly predate mound construction.

Public Structures

Three sets of public buildings were located beneath the mound at Town Creek. These structures were presumably the locus of political activities within the earliest Mississippian community at the site. The first set of public buildings consisted of a larger rectangular structure (Structure 4a) and a smaller square one (Structure 24). Structure 4a contained at least four burials, a child and three adult women. Three of the burials were associated with artifacts, which included marine shell fragments and beads, stone beads, and a ceramic pot. Structure 24 contained three flexed burials on its north side and a possible fourth burial that contained only a few human bones on its south side. The three definite burials were all older adults at least 35 years old at the time of death. Two of these individuals were males and the third possibly a female. One of the males was buried with a number of small columella beads and six bone needles that have been interpreted as a ceremonial skin scratcher like those used by Historic native groups (Coe 1995:240). These were items used by ritual practitioners for blood-letting in curing rituals (Culin 1975:580–581 and Plate 14; Hudson 1976:415–417; Mooney 1890:121–122; Speck 1979: Figure 40; Swanton 1979:564).

The second early Town Creek phase public building was the earth-embanked Structure 4b. Two burials were located within this building. One of these interments was the extended burial of an adult female and the other a child who was buried with six shell pendants.

The third cohort of early Town Creek phase public buildings consisted of Structures 23a and 23c. These were the public buildings in use immediately prior to mound construction. Structures 23a and 23c were paired structures consisting of a square earth-embanked building connected to a large, relatively lightly constructed rectangular building. The burials of four infants were located in these structures, but they did not contain any adult burials. Three of the infant burials were located in the northeast corner of Structure 23c, adjacent to an interior roof support and a line of postholes forming a wall. The fourth was located in the line of postholes forming the west wall of Structure 23a. The fact that they may have been the only burials, coupled with their location within the buildings—adjacent to a roof support post and, in one case, in a line of wall posts—suggests that these burials may represent ritual interments, possibly related to the construction of these structures. The association of infant sacrifices with Mississippian public buildings has been documented in the archaeological and ethnohistoric records (Blitz 1993a:88–89; Butler 1934:41; Kenton 1927:341, 431; McWilliams 1988:90, 93–95; Peebles and Kus 1977:439–440). The situation at Town Creek is not as clear-cut as these examples, though, and is open to alternative interpretations.

Small Circular Structures

Seventy-two individuals were buried within Small Circular Structures at Town Creek. The general pattern is that burials were placed in a cluster near the

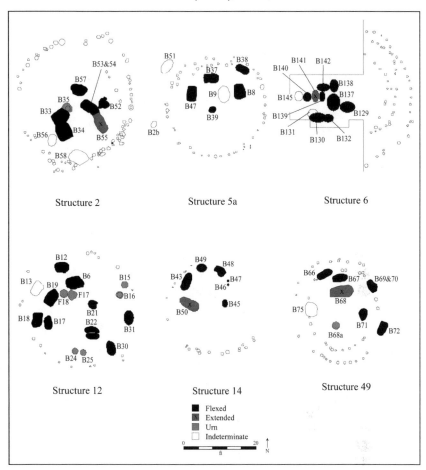

Figure 4.1. Burials in Small Circular Structures.

center of each structure (Figure 4.1). All age-sex categories are represented (Table 4.1), which is consistent with their having been used by an entire family group. The representative demographic profile of Small Circular Structures, coupled with their size and ubiquity, suggests that these were domestic structures.

Most individuals within Small Circular Structures were buried in a flexed position (n=48). The exceptions were several urn (n=8) and extended (n=4) burials. Urn burials are interments in which infants were placed in large complicated-stamped or textile-impressed jars that were buried in pits in structure floors (see Coe 1952:309; Ferguson 1971:206). In at least one case, a ceramic bowl had been inverted over the mouth of the jar and used as a

Table 4.1. Burials by time period and structure type

	Youth			Adult											Miscellaneous	Total
	Children[a]	Adolescent	Indeterminate	Young (ind. sex)	Young female	Young male	Mature (ind. sex)	Mature female	Mature male	Older (ind. sex)	Older female	Older male	Male (ind. age)	Indeterminate age/sex	Indeterminate age/sex	
Late Woodland																
Structure 18	—	2	—	—	—	2	—	—	2	—	—	1	—	—	—	7
Mississippian																
Small Circular	10	12	3	6	9	5	2	6	5	—	6	5	—	—	3	72
Enclosed Circular	24	10	—	2	4	6	2	4	4	2	6	11	1	1	3	80
Large Rectangular	1	4	—	2	3	—	—	—	1	2	2	—	—	1	—	14
Small Rectangular	—	1	—	—	—	—	1	—	—	—	—	—	—	—	1	2
Medium Rectangular	1	1	—	—	—	—	—	—	—	—	—	—	—	—	—	3
Premound Public (Mg2)	6	—	—	—	1	—	—	3	—	—	1	2	—	1	—	14
Mound Summit (Mg2)	—	—	—	2	1	1	—	—	—	—	—	—	—	1	—	5
Enclosure 1 (Mg3)	4	1	—	5	3	—	—	3	—	—	—	1	—	2	2	21
Unassigned Burial Clusters	4	4	—	2	—	1	1	—	—	—	1	1	—	1	1	16
Protohistoric																
Burial Clusters 14 and 20	3	1	—	2	1	2	—	—	—	—	2	—	—	—	3	14
Total	53	36	3	21	22	17	6	16	12	2	18	21	1	7	13	248

[a] Age classes are children (0–5 years), adolescents (6–14), young adults (15–24), mature adults (25–34), and older adults (35+) (see Boudreaux 2005:270).

cover. It is likely that more, possibly all, urn burials also included an inverted bowl as a lid but that these were not preserved in plowed contexts. Urn burials were found in three of the excavated Small Circular Structures (Structures 2, 12, and 49).

In four of the six excavated Small Circular Structures (Structures 2, 6, 14, and 49), the extended burial of an adult was located within the cluster of flexed burials. Thus, it seems clear that one adult in each domestic structure was distinguished at the time of death with a unique burial position. Burial Cluster 40 conforms to this pattern as well. One exception to this pattern is Structure 5a, but position was not recorded in the field for the central burial in this structure, so it could well have contained an extended burial. The other exception is Structure 12, a Small Circular Structure located next to the river. This structure was superimposed by at least two other structures and a large, shallow pit, so it is possible that it also contained an extended burial but that it was destroyed by subsequent activities.

Artifacts were associated with 22 of the burials in Small Circular Structures. Columella beads were the most ubiquitous. Noteworthy occurrences include several copper fragments in Structure 5a and a Pine Island style gorget (see Brain and Phillips 1996:28–30) in Structure 14. The most distinctive artifact associated with a burial in a Small Circular Structure was a copper axe found with the extended burial of an older adult male located within Structure 14. Five of the infants in urn burials were associated with artifacts other than the urns themselves. Most of these were columella beads. The one urn burial with more than shell beads was one within Structure 49 that included a Pine Island tyle shell gorget and a quartz crystal.

Late Town Creek–Leak Phase

The late Town Creek–Leak phase community consisted of public buildings on the mound summit, a special area next to the Little River that was set apart by a rectangular enclosure, and a plaza that was surrounded by Enclosed Circular, Large Rectangular, and Small Rectangular Structures. The burials from this phase largely or wholly postdate mound construction.

Summit Structures

Two sets of buildings located on two different mound summits were excavated. Each set consisted of two small, square structures joined by an entrance trench. It is likely that these two buildings were located behind a large, arborlike rectangular structure located on the plaza side of the summit. The northern building (Structure 45a) in the earlier set of structures contained two flexed burials that were located next to a central hearth (Figure 4.2). An additional grave-shaped pit was located nearby, but it did not contain any bone. Both of the individuals in Structure 45a were young adults. Sex could

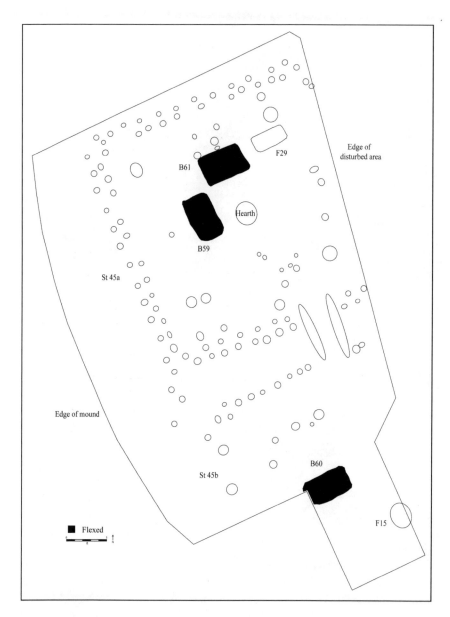

Figure 4.2. Burials associated with Structures 45a and 45b on the mound summit.

not be determined for one of them. This person was buried with two pieces of quartz crystal. The other burial was that of a male who was interred with six different types of artifacts. These included a piece of red ochre, two projectile points, and a number of columella beads, several of which were made of large, relatively unmodified portions of shell. This individual was also buried with three circular mica ornaments that were in the form of an excised cross. Two piles of small pebbles located in the grave were interpreted as the remains of rattles. The southern building (Structure 45b) in the earlier set of summit structures contained one flexed burial and an empty circular pit. The burial was an adult whose age and sex could not be determined. This person was associated with fragments of mica and a pile of pebbles that indicated the presence of a rattle.

Only two burials were associated with the two structures on the later summit. The northern structure (Structure 46a) contained several large and small empty pits as well as a bundle burial located near the entrance (Figure 4.3). This individual was a young adult female who was buried with a marine shell pin. The only feature that was not a posthole identified within the southern structure (Structure 46b) was the bundle burial of a young adult whose sex could not be determined. This person was not buried with any artifacts.

Two bundle burials were associated with the two structures on the uppermost intact mound summit (Structures 46a and 46b). These are different from the two structures (Structures 45a and 45b) on the preceding mound summit, which contained only primary interments. This difference could represent a change in the mortuary ritual associated with mound-summit burials where earlier summit burials were primary interments and later ones were subjected to postmortem processing and then reburied as a skeletonized bundle. Alternatively, it is possible that this apparent pattern of change is an artifact of the excavations. Although the burials on the mound were attributed to different summits, it could have been that the excavators were not able to attribute burials accurately to either of the two superimposed summits. Earthen mounds are complex to excavate stratigraphically because they consist of a number of different fills. At Town Creek, sorting out the stratigraphy would have been further complicated by the fact that the previously disturbed mound was excavated by an unskilled labor force. Thus, it may be better to think of the summit burials as a single group. The features located on the two summits, when considered together, include empty pits, primary burials, and secondary burials. This assemblage of features may represent a mortuary program in which individuals were interred on the summit and exhumed after the remains had become skeletonized. These remains were possibly stored for a period of time in aboveground containers such as a box or a basket and then reinterred as a bundle in the structure floor (see Brown 1971:105).

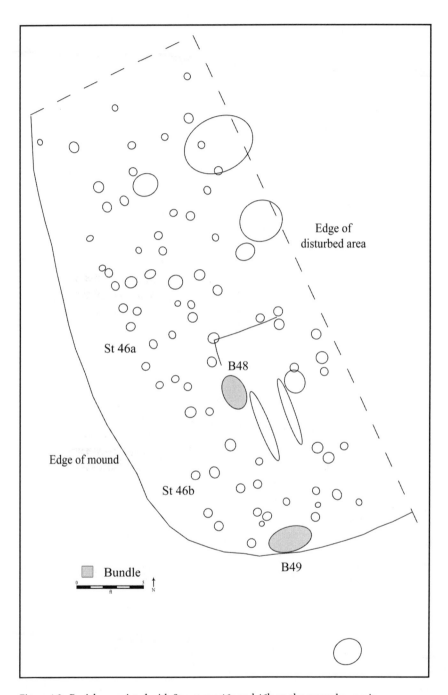

Figure 4.3. Burials associated with Structures 46a and 46b on the mound summit.

Public Structures Next to the River

Several superimposed structures, a number of burials, and a rectangular en-closure were located in the area next to the Little River across from the mound (Figure 4.4). Enclosure 1 encompasses Structure 51 as well as two burial clus-ters. Burial Cluster 11 is located on its north side and Burial Cluster 13 on its south side. These burial clusters included 16 human burials. Interestingly, Burial Cluster 11 also contained the urn burial of a dog. Both clusters consist of several burials around the central burial of an adult woman associated with unique artifacts. All age classes are represented in the burial clusters within Enclosure 1. The adults in these clusters whose sex could be determined were female (n=6), with one exception of an older adult male in Burial Cluster 11. With the exception of a single extended burial, the individuals in these two clusters were buried in a flexed position (n=10).

Seven of the 17 individuals in Burial Clusters 11 and 13 were associated with artifacts. These include some of the most distinctive artifacts found at Town Creek. The central interment in Burial Cluster 11 is the flexed burial of a young adult woman who was associated with three projectile points and a rattle. This woman was also buried with four conch-shoulder gorgets—ornaments made from the curved portion of shell that encompasses the spire, shoulder, and body portions of a conch (Boudreaux 2005:295). The remains of an infant were located near this woman's feet and a skull near her head. It is not known if these three burials were intentionally associated or if they are a palimpsest of unrelated burials. The flexed burial of another young adult fe-male in Burial Cluster 11 was associated with fragments of marine shell and a section of a large complicated-stamped jar. The central interment in Burial Cluster 13 is the extended burial of a mature adult woman who was interred next to the south wall of Enclosure 1 and oriented perpendicular to it. In ad-dition to her unique location and burial position, this woman was associ-ated with 98 columella beads, 4 bracket-style marine shell earpins (see Brain and Phillips 1996:362), and a copper-covered wooden earspool. Another in-dividual in Burial Cluster 13 with a unique artifact is the flexed burial of a young adult woman who was interred with two disks made of polished non-local stone that may have been ear ornaments. A child burial was associated with two ceramic disks, a polished stone disk, two copper-covered wooden earspools, and a rattle.

Five individuals were buried inside Structure 51. Burials were aligned to the wall of the structure and were arranged in a square near its center. The buri-als for which position could be determined were flexed, and those for which age could be determined were young adults. Sex could be determined for only one individual, an adult male. Three of the burials were associated with arti-

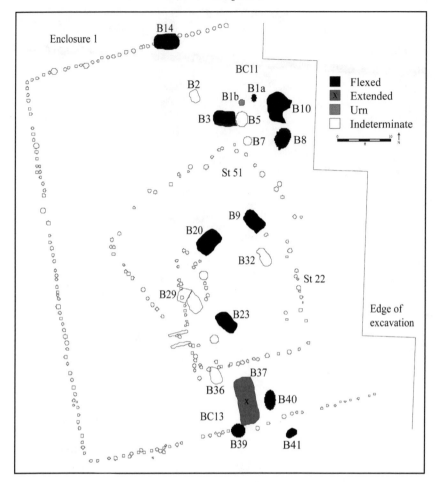

Figure 4.4. Burials associated with Enclosure 1 and Structure 51.

facts. The flexed burial of a young adult located on the east side of the structure contained a large columella bead, and a large stone had been placed near the person's head. The flexed burial of a young adult located on the west side of the structure was associated with 16 relatively unmodified columella beads and fragments of mica. The flexed burial of an adult male was located near the center of Structure 51 and exactly at the center of Enclosure 1. In addition to being clearly buried in relation to prominent public structures, this person was associated with one of the most diverse and unusual burial assemblages at Town Creek. This man's burial included one columella bead, four projectile points, mica fragments, a pottery pipe, a rattle, and a raccoon skull.

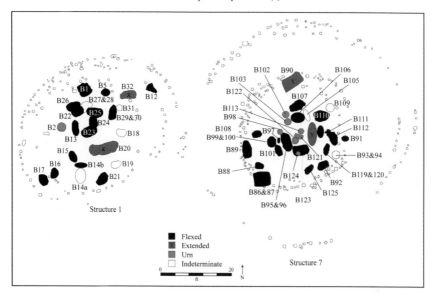

Figure 4.5. Burials in Enclosed Circular Structures.

Enclosed Circular Structures

Eighty individuals were buried in the two excavated Enclosed Circular Structures. Burials were located in a dense cluster at the center of each structure (Figure 4.5). They were entirely within the inner circular pattern for Structure 7 and mostly within the inner circular pattern for Structure 1. All age-sex categories are represented in these structures. Most of the individuals in these structures were buried in a flexed position (n=45). Urn burials that contained infants were placed near the center of the burial cluster in both structures, seven in Structure 7 and one in Structure 1. Several of these burials also had a bowl inverted over the top of the jar. Similar to Small Circular Structures, both of the Enclosed Circular Structures also contained extended burials. Unlike Small Circular Structures, though, each Enclosed Circular structure contained two individuals buried in an extended position. In each case, one person was buried near the center of the cluster of burials and the other on the periphery. Structure 1 also contained a bundle burial and a disarticulated burial.

Twenty-three of the individuals buried in Enclosed Circular Structures were associated with artifacts. Columella beads were the most common type of artifact. Two children in Structure 7 were associated with a number of marginella shell beads (n=63 and 1,655), which suggests that they were buried with a beaded garment. Five of the eight urn burials included beads, four in-

dividuals with shell beads and one associated with a bone bead. Copper fragments were found with two individuals, the bundle burial of a young adult
female in Structure 1 and the flexed burial of an older adult male in Structure 7. Two children in Structure 7 were each buried with two conch-shoulder
gorgets.

Large Rectangular Structures

Structures 27 and 30b are the only Large Rectangular Structures that were excavated at Town Creek (Figure 4.6). Structure 27 represents the eastern portion of a Large Rectangular Structure located on the northwest side of the
plaza. The western part of this structure extends into an unexcavated part of
the site. Nine individuals were buried in the eastern part of this structure, and
their graves are, for the most part, widely spaced across the structure's interior.
Two adolescents were buried in a flexed position in the northeast corner, and
a child was buried in a flexed position in the southeast corner. Two burials of
young adult females were located near what was probably the center of the
structure. Also near the structure's center was a large square pit that contained
the disarticulated remains of four individuals—an adult, a young adult, and
two adolescents. A deer jaw and a pottery disk in this pit are the only burial
associations within this structure, although these artifacts could have been
incidental inclusions within the jumble of bones in this pit. Based on Structure 27, it could have been that the activities that took place in at least some
Large Rectangular Structures included rituals involving the manipulation of
skeletal remains or their reburial.

Four burials were widely spaced across the interior of Structure 30b, and
another possibly related burial was located just outside of the building. The
interior burials were all flexed. They consisted of two older adult females, a
young adult female, and a young adult of indeterminate sex. The only associated artifact was a quartzite pebble with one of the older adult women. The
exterior burial was a mature adult male in the flexed position who was not
buried with any artifacts.

MORTUARY PATTERNS

In this section, evidence is discussed pertaining to the manifestation of leadership roles in the Mississippian mortuary record and how these roles changed
during this period. Change will be explored by comparing premound-
construction and postmound-construction contexts. The premound data
come from the early Town Creek phase submound, public buildings and Small
Circular Structures. Postmound data come from late Town Creek and Leak
phase contexts: the mound-summit structures, Enclosed Circular Structures,

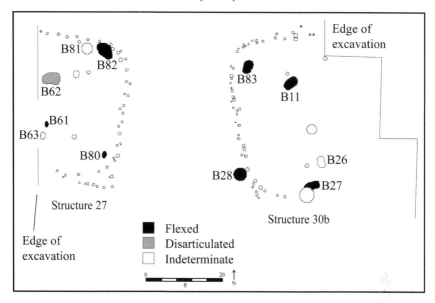

Figure 4.6. Burials in Large Rectangular Structures.

Large Rectangular Structures, Small Rectangular Structures, and contexts located within Enclosure 1. Enclosed Circular Structures, while problematic because they appear to be essentially Small Circular Structures that were used later as cemeteries and their burial populations may represent multiple phases, will be considered as part of the postmound sample for comparative purposes because the ultimate use of these structures—as indicated by pottery and their distribution relative to Large Rectangular Structures—occurred after the mound was in use.

Premound Mortuary Data

The earliest Mississippian public buildings at Town Creek were a large rectangular structure (Structure 4a) and a small square structure (Structure 24) oriented the same way and located next to each other on the western edge of the plaza. Structure 4a was associated with the burials of at least three and possibly four adult women and one adolescent. The exclusive association of adult women with a public building and the absence of adult men is an uncommon situation in the Mississippian world (Sullivan 2001:110). It is not what one would expect from reading the ethnohistoric record in which men predominantly—and in some communities exclusively—met in councils to make political decisions (Braund 1999:145; Lefler 1967:49; Sattler 1995:220; Speck 1979:120; Waselkov and Braund 1995:62, 105, 149; Worth 1998:88,

94). Indeed, it is a very different pattern from what has been observed archaeologically at other Southeastern sites. At the late Mississippian and Protohistoric Qualla phase Coweeta Creek site in western North Carolina, Rodning (1999:12, 2001:94–97) has documented a pattern in which men were overwhelmingly associated with public buildings and women with domestic ones.

If males generally were the preferred leaders in Mississippian and Historic period communities (see Worth 1998:88), why are only women interred in one of the early Town Creek phase public buildings? Ethnohistoric accounts clearly indicate that women played prominent social and political roles in many native communities as the leaders of households, kin groups, and clans (Sullivan 2001:110). Also, women could be political leaders outright (Clayton et al. 1993:278; Worth 1998:86). Even if they did not occupy a formal political role, there is ample evidence that women as clan and lineage leaders could influence the male-dominated realms of warfare and politics (Perdue 1998:52; Sattler 1995:222). In addition, it was through female ancestors that kin-group membership was determined among most Southeastern Indians. Being a member of a kin group was essential to participating in community life because kin groups—in the form of clans and local lineages—were directly associated with rights and obligations within the community (Hudson 1976:189; Knight 1990:6, 10; Perdue 1998:24, 46, 47). The fact that access to community life was determined by kinship through women is clearly demonstrated by the practice of adoption in which it was women who decided if prisoners would be killed to atone for the deaths of clan members or adopted to replace a member and given full rights within the clan (Perdue 1998:53–54; Sattler 1995:222). Clearly, participation in society was made possible by one's membership in a lineage through a relationship, either natal or adoptive, with a woman (Perdue 1998:54). Thus, women must have held a great deal of power and influence in native communities because they provided access to the kin-groups that constituted much of the social and political structure of these communities. The presence of women exclusively in early Town Creek phase public buildings suggests that women played a prominent role in the community's political decision-making process at that time. The fact that women's political power within native Southeastern societies likely derived from leadership roles within kin groups suggests that community political leadership and kin-group leadership were inextricably related during the early Town Creek phase.

Another early Town Creek phase public building (Structure 24), which was contemporary with the one associated with the adult females, contained only older adults—all three of whom were at least 35 years or older at the time of death. Two of these individuals are males, the other female. The association of older adults with a public building is consistent with observations about Southeastern societies in the ethnohistoric record. Older individuals, especially those who had distinguished themselves through their achievements, were esteemed in native communities (Gearing 1958:1149; Lefler 1967:43; Sattler 1995:225; Waselkov and Braund 1995:118). A recurrent feature of political organization among Historic groups was a council of older adults, primarily men, that advised the chief (Hudson 1976:225; Muller 1997:83). The presence at Town Creek of a public building with only older adults during the early Town Creek phase indicates that older individuals were esteemed at a community-wide level and that these individuals probably participated in the political process at this time.

Small Circular Structures are clearly distinct when compared to early Town Creek phase public buildings. In contrast to the more restricted demographic profiles of the submound public buildings, all five age classes and both sexes are represented in the burials found in Small Circular Structures. The more representative nature of the demographic profiles of these structures suggests that burial within them was open to all members of the social group. The burial of infants in urns occurred in several Small Circular Structures while this treatment was absent in public buildings. This suggests that placing children in urns was an important part of household or kin-group mortuary rituals but that it was not a part of the rituals that took place in public buildings.

Seven individuals in the early Town Creek phase community are distinctive because they were buried in an extended burial position, but it is difficult to determine the status signified by this treatment. Four extended burials were found in Small Circular Structures, another in a burial cluster, and two in the premound public building Structure 4a. Nearly all of the individuals buried in the extended position during the early Town Creek phase were adults (n=6). There are two indications that the extended burial position marks an important status. First, with the exception of the public building Structure 4a, only one individual per structure or burial cluster was treated in this way. Second, extended burials were generally placed in a central location within an architectural element. Whatever the status may have been, it does not seem to have been determined by sex because two of the early Town Creek phase extended burials are males and four are females. The six adult burials represent all three stages of adulthood. Whatever this status may have been, it was signified by burial position and location but not by durable objects; only 3 of the 10 extended adult burials had artifacts. Interestingly, two of these (Burials 37 and 50/Mg3) had some of the most unusual artifacts at the site, including polished columella beads, a copper axe, shell ear pins, and a copper-covered wooden ear spool.

The presence of no more than one extended adult burial in each Small Circular Structure, burial cluster, and Structure 4a suggests that only one adult throughout the use-life of the structure or burial space could occupy the particular role manifested by this burial position. If Small Circular Structures were used and rebuilt in place for 20 to 30 years, as may have been the case with structures at other Mississippian sites (see Hally 2002:91), then perhaps one person in a generation occupied the role signified by an extended burial position. The distribution of extended burials across the site may indicate that the status marked by this burial position existed in many of the social groups that constituted the Mississippian community at Town Creek, perhaps in each household or matrilineage. It is possible that the extended burials in Small Circular Structures and burial clusters are those of important or senior lineage members.

The distribution of early Town Creek phase adult burials by NAT is continuous. Assuming that there was a correlation between the number of artifact types interred with a person and the number of different roles they played within the community, then there are no individuals that clearly stand out as potential community leaders based on NAT. A slightly higher percentage of the burials in premound public buildings (43 percent) during the early Town Creek phase were associated with artifacts than were those in domestic contexts (28 percent) (Boudreaux 2005:413–419). If burial goods marked some status held or role played by an individual during life, the fact that individuals placed in public buildings were more likely to have associated artifacts than individuals placed in the village is consistent with the former having played more prominent roles in the community than the latter.

It is interesting that the individuals buried in the early Town Creek phase public structures are not distinguished by either the quality or quantity of their associated artifacts. The one exception, an older adult male, was buried with a tool that is similar to the ceremonial scratchers that were used during the Historic period (Coe 1995:240), indicating that this person may have been a ritual practitioner (see Hudson 1976:415–416; Swanton 1979:564). Interestingly, there was an association in some Historic communities between ritual bloodletting with scratchers and leadership (Lefler 1967:49; Speck 1979:121; Waselkov and Braund 1995:71). Also, bone tools that may have been used for bloodletting or tattooing have been associated with high-status males at Koger's Island, a late fourteenth- or early fifteenth-century Mississippian cemetery in the Tennessee Valley of North Alabama (Dye 2000:8). In addition, observations by Bartram (Waselkov and Braund 1995:122, 144) suggest that tattooing may have been related to status in some Southeastern groups during the late eighteenth century.

Generally, it is the placement of some early Town Creek phase individuals within public buildings, rather than their grave accompaniments, that is most distinctive. This practice resembles Historic Cherokee communities in which burials of community leaders are distinguished only by their placement in the vicinity of the townhouse (Sullivan 1995:117). In contrast, there is an older adult male in the early Town Creek phase village who was buried with a copper axe, the only such artifact at Town Creek. This type of artifact is distinctive in Mississippian contexts because it is generally associated with mound burials in conjunction with other unusual artifacts that are often made from exotic materials (Brain and Phillips 1996:362). Copper axes have been interpreted as symbols of political authority at other Mississippian sites (Brain and Phillips 1996:362; Fox 2004; Peebles 1971:82; Scarry 1992:178–179). If this was also the case at Town Creek, then, based on artifacts, one of the likely political leaders of the early Town Creek phase community was not buried in a public building but was instead interred in what appears to be a typical house.

The overall political organization of the early Town Creek phase community seems relatively diffuse, spread among many individuals and multiple social groups. These groups are represented by the adult women buried in one public building, the older adult men and women buried in another public building, and the older adult man buried with a copper axe in a house. The association of adult women with one public building and older adults with another implies that both groups participated in the political process. If the political power of adult women in some Native communities was based on their role as clan or lineage leaders (Perdue 1998:41; Rodning 2001:96; Sattler 1995:222; Sullivan 2001:107), then the inclusion of adult women in a public building at Town Creek may reflect their status as representatives of their kin groups. If the older adults represent a group of esteemed individuals that served as a council, a common political feature in Southeastern societies (Braund 1999:144; Hudson 1976:225; Lefler 1967:204; Muller 1997:81; Moore 1988:32; Waselkov and Braund 1995:118), then it seems that one could also participate in the political process based on lifetime achievements. The representation of all three adult age classes in premound public buildings indicates that the political process involved individuals from all stages of adulthood. Early Town Creek phase public contexts contain an equal representation of mature adults and older adults while young adults are the least well represented. This suggests that adults in the latter two stages of their lives were preferred for positions of leadership during the early Town Creek phase, which is consistent with the importance of achievement as a factor in filling community leadership roles at this time.

It is clear from the ethnohistoric record that political relationships within and among kin groups were a major component of a community's political structure (Hudson 1976:184–185; Knight 1990; Muller 1997:190–192; Sullivan 2001:105). The extended burial position of one of the adult women in an early Town Creek phase public building may also speak to a relationship between kinship and politics. The overall distribution of extended burials and their location near the center of circular structures indicate that individuals buried in this way were distinctive within their kin groups. If the extended burial position signifies some important kin-group status, then the presence of an extended burial—which may represent the leader of a preeminent kin group—in an early Town Creek phase public building may indicate the importance of kinship within the leadership process at this time. It may have been that in addition to lifetime achievements, the representation of kin groups was an important element of the early Town Creek phase political process. Also, it is likely that the leaders of households and lineages, perhaps those individuals distinguished by the extended burial position and placement near the center of household burial clusters, also participated in community politics during the early Town Creek phase.

The fact that, based on artifacts, an individual who likely was a community leader, the man with the copper axe, was buried in a house rather than a public building is also consistent with the importance of kinship in the early Town Creek phase political process in that at least some community leader's political roles were equal or even subservient to their roles within their own households. Perhaps a formal, institutionalized role of community-wide political leader did not exist at this time. The fact that the individual with the copper axe was an older adult speaks to the relationship between lifetime achievement and leadership during the early Town Creek phase.

The mortuary data suggest that political power was shared among multiple contexts and by multiple social groups during the early Town Creek phase. There is no indication from the archaeological data that any one of these groups—the women in the public buildings, the older adults in the public buildings, the older adult male with the copper axe, or the adult men and women placed at the center of household burial clusters—played a more prominent role in the community's political decision-making process than did any other group. The seemingly diffuse nature of political power within the early Mississippian community at Town Creek is consistent with the concept of heterarchy, a form of societal organization in which power is shared or counterpoised among multiple groups (Crumley 1987, 1995). Heterarchy, which was introduced as an alternative, or complement, to the concept of hierarchy, describes situations in which social and political relationships are complex but not necessarily hierarchical (Crumley 1995:3). Political decision-making within the early Town Creek phase community may have consisted of negotiations among kin-group leaders, a council of older adults, and an individual recognized as a community leader or chief. Political power also could have been situational, with one group holding more sway under certain conditions, such as at ritual events or during times of war (Knight 1990:6; Sullivan 2001:104).

Postmound Mortuary Data

Any discussion of the burials associated with mound-summit structures is complicated by the fact that the eastern half of the mound, and any burials that may have been associated with its buildings, had been destroyed by relic collectors prior to the beginning of professional research at Town Creek. It is possible that there were not any burials in this portion of the mound. An account of the drag-pan-and-mule excavations at Town Creek did not mention the disturbance of burials (Coe 1995:303), although this work clearly was not conducted under controlled circumstances. Burials were not located in the eastern premound building at Town Creek or in the eastern building on the various summits of the Dyar Mound (Smith 1994). High-status burials were located in the eastern building on the summit of Mound A at the Toqua site (Polhemus 1987). Unfortunately, there is no way to know for sure if burials were or were not present in the eastern portion of the mound at Town Creek. Although the interpretations offered here obviously would benefit from a complete knowledge of the archaeological record and burial population of the mound at Town Creek, it is unlikely that these interpretations would be fundamentally altered by additional data from missing portions of the mound.

The demographic profiles of public buildings located in mound-summit contexts and next to the Little River are less representative than those of other structure types. This is consistent with the idea that access to public buildings was limited in some way to a subset of the community. Public buildings, both in the area of the mound and next to the river, exhibited five or fewer age-sex classes. The less representative nature of the burials in the mound area is consistent with proscriptions about access to public buildings and mound summits that were documented among Historic groups (Kenton 1927:427; McWilliams 1988:92; Sattler 1995:220; Waselkov and Braund 1995:102, 149; Worth 1998:88). The fact that all age and sex categories are not represented in the burials in the public structures next to the river is consistent with the fact that this area was set off by an enclosure which likely served as a barrier to access (Blitz 1993a:84; DePratter 1983:118; Holley 1999:29; Larson 1971:59; Payne 1994:223).

The more restricted nature of the demographic profiles of public buildings contrasts with Enclosed Circular Structures and Large Rectangular Structures, where all five age classes and both sexes are represented. This suggests that burial within these structures was open to all members of a social group regardless of age. Because there are multiple examples of each of these structure types located at Town Creek, it seems likely that Enclosed Circular and Large Rectangular Structures were used by kin-based groups, most likely clan-based matrilineages. When both age and sex are considered, all classes are represented in Enclosed Circular Structures. Large Rectangular Structures, in contrast, are less representative, which suggests that access to them may have been limited to a subset of the kin-based group. The burial of infants in urns occurred in Enclosed Circular Structures, but urn burials are absent in clearly public spaces such as the mound-summit public buildings, as well as in contexts associated with Enclosure 1 and Structure 51 next to the river. If placing children in urns was an important part of kin-group mortuary rituals but not something that took place in public buildings, then the absence of urn burials in Large Rectangular Structures is consistent with the idea that these were public structures that were possibly associated with individual kin groups.

As was the case with Small Circular Structures, some individuals within Enclosed Circular Structures were buried in an extended position. In the case of Enclosed Circular Structures, though, two individuals within each structure were distinguished in this way. If the status signified by the extended burial position was filled by one person per generation in each group, then the presence of two extended burials in each of the Enclosed Circular Structures would be consistent with the use-life of these structures having been longer than the use-life of Small Circular Structures.

An examination of the people buried in the mound during the late Town Creek–Leak phases suggests a somewhat different political situation than that of the premound community. The mound-summit burials for which age could be determined were young adults (n=4). This pattern contrasts with premound public buildings, where young adults represented the lowest percentage of any age category. If the mound was the locus of political decision-making within the community, and if all of the mound-summit burials were preserved at Town Creek, then the exclusive presence of young adults in summit buildings could indicate a change in the nature of leadership that followed the construction of the mound.

An important manifestation of political power in Mississippian communities would have been the placement of a residence on the summit of a platform mound, the community's symbol of political authority (Anderson 1994:119–120, 1999:220; DePratter 1983:207–208; Milanich et al. 1997:118; Rudolph 1984:40; Steponaitis 1986:386). If the mound had been used as a residence, it could be expected that the demographic profiles of the mound-summit burials would be relatively inclusive, possibly similar to that associated with Small Circular Structures, which probably were houses. Instead, only one age class is represented on the mound summit, and subadults are completely absent. The more restrictive demographic profile associated with the mound summit is not consistent with the summit having served as a residence for a family.

The placement of an enclosure that encompassed a number of burials on the eastern side of the plaza is a significant change that occurred during the late Town Creek–Leak phase. Enclosure 1 includes individuals of both sexes and all five age classes, suggesting that it may have been open to burial from all members of a kin group. Young adults (n=8) are the most common age group represented, constituting 67 percent of the adult burials for which age could be determined. If Enclosure 1 was a kin-group cemetery, the facts that the burials were set apart by a distinctive rectangular enclosure that was placed across the plaza from the mound in an area of public architecture suggests that the kin group buried in this prominent place occupied a preeminent social position within the community. A frequently cited attribute of the social structure of some Southeastern communities is that clan-based matrilineages were ranked relative to each other (Knight 1990:8; Sattler 1995:224). It may have been the case at Town Creek during the late Town Creek–Leak phases that one social group, perhaps a kin-based matrilineage, was able to become distinguished and occupy a preeminent position within the community.

One possible explanation for the association of young adults with the mound and the rectangular enclosure is that leadership following mound construction may have been associated with risky behaviors that might lead to death at an early age. This could mean that participation in warfare was a prominent activity for leaders at this time because young adulthood for males was the time when they were most likely to distinguish themselves in warfare (Sullivan 2001:124). The presence of young adult females is more perplexing, though, because the avenues available for women to enhance their status through achievement likely were open during later stages of life (Eastman 2001:73; Sullivan 2001:120). Alternatively, while lifetime achievement may have been an important factor affecting leadership status prior to mound construction, it is possible that leadership following mound construction was closely linked to current or recent achievement, with individuals being eligible for such positions during a period of their lives when they would have been heavily involved in the community's economy, politics, social life, and military defense.

One of the major differences thought to have existed between the political organization of Mississippian and other societies in the Southeast is a transition from informal leadership positions, which were based primarily on the charisma and ability of a singular individual who built and maintained a following, to a formally defined office of leadership, which existed independently of any one person (Scarry 1996:4; Steponaitis 1986:983). The absence

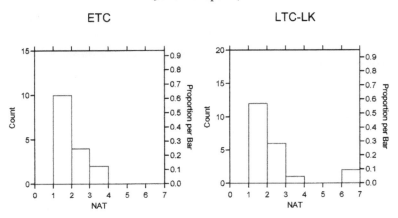

Figure 4.7. Histograms of NAT for early Town Creek and late Town Creek–Leak phase burials with grave goods.

in the mound of individuals from age categories other than young adult implies that following mound construction, the status of community leader may not have been held for life. Perhaps political leaders gave way to younger rivals at some point, and it was only those individuals who died while occupying the status of leader who were eligible for mound burial (see Driscoll 2002:25–26). This is consistent with the idea that an office of "community leader" existed at Town Creek after the mound was built.

It was after the mound was built that some individuals became more distinctive based on where and with what they were buried. All adults during the early Town Creek phase had a NAT value of three or less. Most adults during the late Town Creek–Leak phases also had a NAT value of three or less, but there were two males buried with six artifact types each that were distinct from all of the others (Figure 4.7). Thus, the postmound pattern seems to have been largely the same as the premound pattern with the critical difference being the addition of two outliers. Assuming that artifact types placed in a burial represent a role played by the individual during life, then the two individuals with the highest NAT values may represent late Town Creek–Leak phase community leaders (see Howell 1995:129, 1996:63; Kintigh 2000:104). This idea is supported by the fact that these two individuals were buried in public spaces, perhaps two of the most exceptional locations in the postmound-construction community. One of these individuals was buried on the mound summit and the other was placed at the center of the rectangular enclosure across the plaza.

It is possible that the two adult men buried with unique artifacts occupied the same leadership role within the late Town Creek–Leak phase community that the man buried with the copper axe did in the early Town Creek phase community. However, the location of the two later burials and the variety of their associated artifacts shows a marked change from the early Town Creek phase pattern in which no individuals were distinguished by their NAT values and in which one of the individuals most likely to represent a community leader based on artifacts was buried in a house rather than a public building. The placement of these men in public places, which implies an association with the whole community, rather than in their houses, which implies a primary association with their own families, is consistent with the idea that following mound construction, the leadership role they occupied was more of an office connected with the political institutions of the town rather than something based solely on the abilities of a singular individual who still had strong ties to his own kin group.

Kinship may have been the dominant organizational principle of the early Town Creek phase community at Town Creek. The placement of burials in the floors of houses shows that individuals were kept with their kin group even in death. The predominance of adult women in public buildings and the burial of a community leader in a domestic building is consistent with the importance of kinship. Kinship continued to be important after the construction of the mound. Family cemeteries that began in earlier stages were maintained throughout the late Town Creek–Leak phases; 70 percent of the burials in public buildings for which sex could be determined are female, and an adult woman within the rectangular enclosure was buried in the extended position—a treatment that may signify that this person occupied a preeminent role within a kin group. However, it seems that there was an additional organizational principle at work during this time, one in which certain individuals were recognized as being first and foremost community leaders and one in which public spaces were at least partially associated with community leaders rather than used predominantly as displays of the importance of kinship and lifetime achievement.

Another change in the use of public space following mound construction has to do with the concentration of unusual artifacts within the two primary public spaces—the mound summit and the rectangular enclosure next to the river. The individuals buried in premound public buildings were mostly indistinguishable with regard to the kinds and quantities of artifacts with which they were associated. There were several notable changes that followed mound construction. One change, as discussed previously, is that the two individuals with the highest NAT values were located in public spaces. A second change has to do with the percentage of burials that contained grave goods. The percentage of burials with grave goods in public spaces during the late Town Creek–Leak phases was higher (52 percent) than in both earlier public space burials (43 percent) and contemporaneous village burials (33 percent). If grave goods can be seen as markers of roles occupied by individuals in life, then the higher percentage of public-space burials with grave goods in postmound-construction contexts could mean that these individuals played a more prominent role in the community at that time than did their contemporaries buried in domestic contexts and than did their early Town Creek phase predecessors. A third change has to do with the kinds of artifacts that were found with burials in public spaces. During the early Town Creek phase, there was no association between the burials in public buildings and unusual artifacts, with the exception of the previously discussed bone scratcher. In contrast, distinctive artifacts during the late Town Creek–Leak phases were found only in burials on the mound summit or within the rectangular enclosure across the plaza (Boudreaux 2005:343; Driscoll 2002:22–23). These distinctive artifacts are mostly made from nonlocal materials and include whole and fragmentary mica objects as well as two types of ear ornament, one made from polished stone and the other from copper-covered wooden discs. The rattle is another distinctive artifact type, the presence of which was inferred by the occurrence of fragments of wood and a cluster of pebbles.

Five of the six individuals buried with these unique artifacts for whom age could be determined were young adults. This is not surprising since the unique artifacts are found only in public buildings, which have a high proportion of young adults. The status signified by these artifacts does not seem to have been linked to sex since they are found with both women and men. The fact that an infant was buried with four types of unique artifacts, which is a relatively rich grave within the Town Creek burial population, suggests that there may have been an ascriptive element to the status signified by these artifacts (see Larson 1971:66).

The types of artifacts found with some of the public-space burials during the late Town Creek–Leak phases can give us insights into the roles that these individuals may have played within their communities. The two most distinctive burials contained both rattles and mica. Rattles were often used among Historic Indians in dances that were a part of social and ritual events (Swanton 1979:626–627). Based on iconographic depictions, artifact associations, and the ethnohistoric record, it is clear that high-status individuals in at least some Mississippian communities played critical roles in community rituals (Blitz 1993a:92; Dye 2000:11; Emerson 1997:258; Kenton 1927:427; Knight 1989a:209; Larson 1957:9, 1989:140; McWilliams 1988:92; Pauketat 1994:183–184). The association of rattles exclusively with public spaces during the late Town Creek–Leak phases at Town Creek and their presence in the burials of community leaders is consistent with this idea. During the late Town Creek–Leak phases, the distribution of mica, which may have been part of regalia worn during rituals (Blitz 1993a:86; Larson 1989:140), is also consistent with the idea that the mound summit and rectangular enclosure at Town Creek contained burials of individuals who played important roles in rituals. In addition, the distinctive burial on the mound also contained a lump of red ochre, a mineral thought to have been important as a pigment in various ritual contexts (Blitz 1993a:86). In addition to mica fragments and a rattle, the distinctive burial at the center of the rectangular enclosure also contained a ceramic pipe and a raccoon skull. Among Historic groups, pipes were an integral part of meetings that took place in public buildings (Waselkov and Braund 1995:50, 72, 102, 104). Regarding the skull, raccoons were frequently depicted in Mississippian iconography (Phillips and Brown 1978:136, 154–155), indicating that they were an important part of the belief system. Interestingly, one of the ways Southeastern Indians used raccoons was to make pouches from their hides (Swanton 1979:250). The presence of a skull is consistent with the fact that the animal's head sometimes figured prominently in the design of a pouch (Swanton 1979:480). The raccoon skull was found near a cluster of pebbles that indicated the presence of a rattle, an item that could have been enclosed in a pouch. Among Southeastern Indians, pouches were an important part of the tool kit used by ritual practitioners and were used to hold a variety of sacred objects (Dye 2000:11; Hudson 1976:370; Moore 1988:42–43; Swanton 1979:477–479). Although the exact significance of the raccoon skull will never be known, the fact that it was from an animal that was depicted in religious art and that it may have been part of a pouch that contained a rattle is consistent with the idea that the man buried at the center of the rectangular enclosure played a prominent role in the ritual life of the postmound-construction community at Town Creek.

CONCLUSIONS

The differences in the composition of the burial populations between premound-construction and postmound-construction public buildings, with an emphasis on older and mature adults in the former and young adults in the latter, coupled with the presence of new artifact types, suggests that the people buried in public spaces during the late Town Creek–Leak phases occupied new social and political roles. Mica artifacts, ear ornaments, and rattles are all artifact types that were not present in the early Town Creek phase community. The presence of nonlocal materials (e.g., copper, mica, nonlocal stone) may have been an attempt to legitimate social and political statuses through ties to the external world. These nonlocal materials not only expressed external contacts in the real world but also could have been used as a metaphor for contact with the supernatural (Helms 1979:110). It has been argued that in many chiefdom-level societies, including those of the Mississippian Southeast, expressing ties with the supernatural was a common strategy for legitimating positions of authority (Earle 1989:85–86, 1997:143–144; Helms 1979:120; Keyes 1994:112; Knight 1989a:209–210). It seems that an early Town Creek phase political organization that was more diffuse and representative and that could still be seen as equal to or less important than family and household ties was replaced by a new form of social and political organization during the late Town Creek–Leak phases. This new organization was one in which some individuals—primarily young adults—were clearly distinct, and their ties to a community-wide status, which seems to have been closely related to ritual activities, were more important than their ties to family and household.

Although the mortuary data from Town Creek indicate that significant social and political changes accompanied mound construction, it is not clear that these changes reflect the centralization of political authority. The political situation of the early Town Creek phase community appears to have been heterarchical, complexly but not hierarchically organized (see Crumley 1995:3). The late Town Creek–Leak phase community had slightly different social and political elements, but these may have been heterarchically arranged as well. As was the case during the early Town Creek phase, multiple social groups seem to have occupied preeminent positions within the late Town Creek–Leak phase community. The people buried in the mound, the rectangular enclosure, the kin-group cemeteries, and the kin-group public buildings may all represent distinctive social groups that constituted the late Town Creek–Leak phase community at Town Creek. The real key to the expression of the centralization of political authority is the placement of a residence on the mound summit, which is not supported by the mortuary data. In Chapter 5, ceramic vessel data will be used to evaluate whether the mound, the locus of political power within the community, was co-opted and used as a residence by an aspiring leader.

5

Vessel Analysis

The earthlodge-to-platform-mound model proposes that changes in Mississippian public architecture reflect a centralization of political power that accompanied the appearance of platform mounds (Anderson 1994:119–120, 1999:220; DePratter 1983:207–208; Rudolph 1984:40). While the mortuary data from Town Creek show that there were changes in the nature of leadership between premound and postmound contexts, it is not clear that these changes reflect the centralization of political authority. In this chapter, ceramic vessel data are used as a proxy to investigate the social and political changes that may have accompanied mound construction at Town Creek. Vessel classes and types are defined, the function of vessel types is inferred (see Hally 1983, 1986; Skibo 1992), and differences among assemblages from different phases and contexts are explored. Vessel data are used to identify domestic and nondomestic assemblages. This is important in regard to the evolution of leadership at Town Creek because the existence of a house on the mound—the probable locus of political power—rather than a nondomestic, public building would suggest that political authority was closely associated with a single person or family (i.e., more centralized) after mound construction.

Vessel data will be used in this chapter to define what constitutes a domestic vessel assemblage at Town Creek, a construct that will be a critical part of evaluating whether the public buildings in the Mound Area were also domestic in nature. Variation within the Town Creek community in the types of food-related activities (e.g., various types of cooking, consumption, serving, processing, storage) being performed should be reflected in differences among contexts in frequencies of vessel types (Blitz 1993b:87–93; Turner and Lofgren 1966; Welch and Scarry 1995:413–414). While the types of activities indicated by a particular vessel assemblage may not always be clear, it is likely that contexts with similar assemblages were associated with similar sets of activities while those with different assemblages were not (see Hally 1984:58–

59). Owing to the variety of activities associated with household production and consumption, domestic vessel assemblages should include a broad range of vessel types and sizes to accomplish diverse tasks (Blitz 1993b:93; Taft 1996:57). In contrast, some Mississippian public buildings probably were associated with more restricted activities such as feasting and large-scale, communal food storage (Blitz 1993a:72; Kenton 1927:341, 430–431; McWilliams 1988:88; O'Neill 1977:244; Taft 1996:56–57). It has been argued that the specialized activity of feasting is reflected by more restricted assemblages in which large vessels, both cooking and serving, and serving vessels are proportionally overrepresented in comparison with domestic assemblages (Blitz 1993a:84–85; Emerson 1997:161; Maxham 2000:348; Taft 1996:67–68; Welch and Scarry 1995:412–414). Feasting also has been attributed to short-term deposits that contain high densities of pottery as well as deposits with a number of large vessel fragments (Pauketat et al. 2002:269).

Vessel data are also used to assess the accessibility of public buildings. If political authority was centralized after mound construction, then fewer people would have been participating in the decision-making process and accessing the public buildings where political decisions were made. Differences in vessel size are important because, assuming that group size and the amount of food consumed were correlated, vessel size—as a proxy for the amount of food cooked and served at one time—should reflect the relative number of people who used a context (see Turner and Lofgren 1966). For public buildings, exploring assemblages by size could indicate the relative size of the group that had access to them. In the case of public buildings in which community-wide decisions were made, knowing the relative size of the group that had access to them could indicate the relative size of the decision-making group.

METHODS

An assemblage of 180 complete or partial Pee Dee vessels from the Town Creek (n=148), Leak (n=25), and Teal (n=7) sites was analyzed in order to identify vessel types and functions (Boudreaux 2005:352). Vessel classes and types were defined largely by shape. These shape-based classes and types are probably related to vessel function because morphological differences can affect a vessel's performance in the manipulation, removal, and heating of vessel contents (Braun 1980:173; Hally 1986:278–280; Henrickson and McDonald 1983:630; Smith 1988:912; Wilson and Rodning 2002:30). The use-alterations identified in the Pee Dee assemblage include scratches and pits on vessel interiors which might be the result of manipulating (i.e., stirring and mixing) vessel contents (Hally 1983:20; Skibo 1992:132–138). Exterior use-alterations include thermal alterations such as soot accumulation, oxidation, and reduction, which were related to the vessel's use over fire, presumably for cooking (Hally 1983:11–12; Skibo 1992:154–162; but see Hally 1983:10). The most common exterior use-alteration was a horizontal pattern of thermal alteration in which bases were sooted, the lower parts of vessels were oxidized, and the upper portions were reduced or sooted.

Orifice diameter was used as a proxy measure for vessel size. While vessel volume would be the appropriate measure of vessel size, complete vessels are rare in archaeological contexts. Instead, orifice diameter can be estimated from more commonly found rim sherds. A correlation between orifice diameter and vessel size has been established for other ceramic assemblages (Whallon 1969:89), including those from other Mississippian sites (Hally 1986:279; Shapiro 1984:705), and it is assumed that such a relationship also exists within the Pee Dee assemblage.

All of the Pee Dee vessels analyzed were either bowls or jars. Within these categories, open and restricted forms were recognized, with the former referring to vessels whose maximum diameter is at the lip and the latter to vessels whose maximum diameter is not at the lip (see Shepard 1957:228). The primary vessel types recognized in the Pee Dee assemblage based on shape were carinated bowls, open bowls, restricted bowls, carinated jars, open jars, and restricted jars (Figure 5.1). Two or three size classes were recognized for nearly every vessel type.

FUNCTION

Patterns of use-alterations and characteristics of vessel profiles are used together to make some inferences about the basic functions of the vessel types identified in the assemblage of whole and partial Pee Dee vessels (see Boudreaux 2005:370). It seems that carinated bowls and restricted bowls were serving vessels. All of these vessels are burnished plain, and none of them shows any thermal use-alterations. Some medium open bowls, those that are burnished plain, appear to have been exclusively serving vessels as well because they also lack thermal use-alterations. Small open jars were possibly cups used as serving vessels for individuals. Small restricted jars and carinated jars that lack thermal use-alterations also may have been small serving vessels, or they could have been used for small-scale storage. Other small restricted jars exhibit thermal use-alterations and were probably used for cooking. Some sooted and thermally altered medium open bowls, those with stamped or textile-impressed surface treatments, appear to have been used for short-term cooking and subsequently for serving. It is possible that some of the larger jars

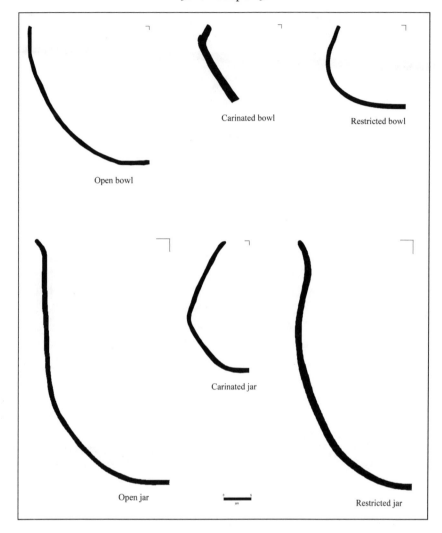

Figure 5.1. Pee Dee vessel types.

were used for storage, but the high proportion of horizontal thermal alterations among medium and large open jars as well as medium restricted jars indicates that larger jars were used predominantly for long-term cooking.

Intrasite Patterns at Town Creek

The ability to make comparisons among spatial and temporal units was determined by where measurable rims were found. Vessels, vessel sections, and rims
used for this analysis came from features within Town Creek and Leak phase

Table 5.1. Percentage of vessel categories by context

Context	Large cooking [a]	Large serving [b]	Small serving and cooking [c]	Number of specimens
Town Creek (all other contexts)	62.8	26.7	10.5	57
Enclosed Circular	46.7	40.0	13.3	15
Large Rectangular	100.0	—	—	2
Level X	44.4	55.6	—	9
Medium Rectangular	66.7	33.3	—	3
Premound Public	57.9	15.8	26.3	19
Riverbank	73.5	20.6	5.9	34
Small Circular	75.0	25.0	—	4

[a] Medium open, large open, medium restricted, and large restricted jars.
[b] Medium carinated, medium open, large open, and restricted bowls.
[c] Small carinated and small open bowls, small open and small restricted jars.

structures, a late Town Creek phase mound-flank midden (Level X) presumably produced by mound-summit activities (see Smith and Williams 1994), and a communal midden located next to the Little River where deposits span the entire Town Creek and Leak phases. While these contexts contained large amounts of pottery overall, sample sizes of specimens from which both vessel shape could be assessed and vessel orifice diameter could be measured or estimated are frustratingly small (see Table 5.1). Because of the small sample sizes, rims are pooled by structure type, and the rims from the submound public buildings are considered as a single analytic unit. All of the rims from premound public buildings either possibly or definitely came from one of the small square structures (i.e., Structures 4b, 23a, or 24).

VESSEL ANALYSIS PATTERNS

Three of the four vessels from Small Circular Structures, which probably represent houses, are restricted jars, a vessel type that the functional analysis shows was used primarily for cooking (Boudreaux 2005:370 and Table 6.4). The riverbank midden assemblage (n=34), which presumably represents a community midden that was produced by the refuse from numerous households (see Schiffer 1987:62), was also dominated by restricted jars (n=25) (Boudreaux 2005:Table 6.4). When all of the vessels from Town Creek that could be assigned to a vessel class are considered (n=148), 58 percent of the assemblage consists of restricted jars (n=86) (Boudreaux 2005:Appendix 2). If most of the assemblages at a site represent domestic ones based on the ubiquity of households in native communities relative to nondomestic contexts, then the fact that most of the assemblages from Town Creek contained a high percentage of jars, especially restricted jars, indicates that cooking was the predominant food-related activity in domestic contexts. The assemblages from Small Circular Structures and the riverbank midden (Table 5.1), which are collectively used to represent the typical domestic assemblage at Town Creek, are characterized by a high percentage (> 70 percent) of large cooking jars, primarily those of the medium restricted type, and a relatively wide range of vessel sizes (Boudreaux 2005:377).

There are three assemblages that are distinctive from the typical domestic assemblage regarding functional types and orifice diameter. They are from Enclosed Circular Structures, the premound public buildings, and the mound-flank midden Level X. Enclosed Circular Structures have a relatively low proportion of large cooking vessels (i.e., medium and large jars), a relatively high proportion of large serving vessels (i.e., medium and large bowls), and some small serving and cooking vessels (i.e., small bowls and jars), which may have been individual serving vessels. The low proportion of large cooking vessels and the high proportion of large serving vessels suggests that there was less emphasis on cooking in Enclosed Circular Structures and more on serving, both individuals and larger groups. Orifice diameters for bowls and jars from Enclosed Circular Structures are not different from those in other contexts (Boudreaux 2005:390), indicating that the groups that did meet in these contexts were probably household-size groups. If Enclosed Circular Structures do represent cemeteries that were used by kin-groups, then the vessel patterns indicate that the consumption of food by household-size groups may have been a part of their burial or mourning rituals.

The premound public buildings have the highest percentage of small serving and cooking vessels, a relatively low percentage of large cooking vessels, and one of the lowest percentages of large serving vessels. The premound assemblage, which comes largely or exclusively from the smallest submound structures, consists of jars that tend to have smaller orifice diameters than those from other contexts. Overall, there is less emphasis on larger-scale cooking in the small premound public buildings and relatively more on serving and possibly cooking for smaller groups. The emphasis in this assemblage on small-group activities suggests that access to the smaller, premound public buildings may have been restricted. Unfortunately, no rims were definitely associated with the large rectangular Structures 4a and 23c, so it is unclear what variation may have existed among the premound public buildings.

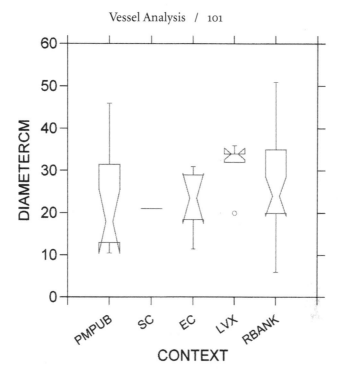

Figure 5.2. Boxplot comparing jar rim diameters (cm) among contexts: premound public buildings, Small Circular Structures, Enclosed Circular Structures, mound-flank midden Level X, and the riverbank midden.

The mound-flank midden (Level X) assemblage is the most distinctive at Town Creek. It contains the lowest percentage of large cooking vessels and the highest percentage of large serving vessels. Small serving and cooking vessels are not present in this midden. Thus, the mound-flank midden vessel assemblage suggests that the mound summit was associated with relatively less cooking and no individual serving but that the serving of groups was more important than in any other context.

A notched boxplot of jar orifice diameters by context (Figure 5.2) shows that jars (n=4) from the mound-flank midden may have been distinctive based on their size. In this figure, the distribution of jar orifice diameter data by context is displayed vertically. The horizontal lines that mark the bottom and top of each box represent the first and third quartiles, respectively, of the distribution, meaning that each box represents half the cases in the distribution (Shennan 1997:45). The most constricted part of each box indicates the sample median, and the notched portions of each box provide a measure of the significance of differences among the values (McGill et al. 1978:14). Notch widths are computed so that those that do not overlap are approximately significantly different at about a 95 percent confidence level (McGill et al. 1978:14). Thus, the fact that the notches of the box for Level X do not overlap with the notches of the boxes representing other samples means that there is a good chance that the true median jar orifice diameter of the mound-flank midden assemblage is larger than the median jar orifice diameter from all other assemblages. The jars from the mound-flank midden are generally larger than 30 cm, while the assemblages from all other contexts are dominated by jars smaller than 30 cm. Furthermore, jars smaller than 20 cm were absent in the mound-flank midden, but they were present in most of the other contexts. The presence of jars that are larger than those found in domestic contexts, the absence of individual serving vessels, and the near absence of smaller jars indicates that the food-related activities that took place on the mound had as their target audience a much larger group than those that took place in all other contexts.

The arrangement of public buildings at Town Creek so that one or more smaller, more substantial buildings were paired with a larger, more ephemeral building is similar to the public buildings in some archaeologically and ethnohistorically documented Cherokee and Creek towns that contained a more substantially constructed "winter council house" as well as a more open, pavilion-like "summer council house" or "public square" (Rodning 2002:12–13; Schroedl 1986:219–224; Waselkov and Braund 1995:102–105). In several Cherokee communities, the summer council house adjoined the winter council house, the two being connected by an enclosed entryway (Rodning 2002: Figure 3; Schroedl 1986:223 and Figure 4.2). Among the Creeks, differences in access existed between the two types of council house. Bartram (Waselkov and Braund 1995:105, Figures 21 and 22) identified one of the buildings on the public square in a Creek town as an open, pavilion-like summer council house where the chiefs, warriors, and citizens of the town assembled to discuss political matters (Waselkov and Braund 1995:104–105). The back of this building was enclosed and accessible only through three small entrances through which one had to crawl on hands and knees. The enclosed back portion of this structure was used to store sacred objects that included rattles, a calumet pipe, and a pot for making medicine (Waselkov and Braund 1995:105). According to Bartram, access to this enclosed area was limited to the chief, the war-chief, and the high priest, and any transgression of this was punishable by death (Waselkov and Braund 1995:105). An adjacent building on the public square was a banqueting hall that accommodated spectators, "particularly at feasts or public entertainments" (Waselkov and Braund 1995:105).

Based on the proscriptions recorded by Bartram and the possible association of mound-summit feasting refuse with a large building at the Dyar Site in

Georgia (Smith 1994:38), there seems to have been a difference in accessibility in some cases between larger and smaller paired Mississippian public buildings, with the larger, more open buildings relatively more accessible and the smaller, more enclosed ones less accessible. While the recovery of measurable rims was such that contemporary large and small public buildings could not be compared, the vessel data suggest that paired large and small public buildings at Town Creek also were more and less accessible, respectively. The vessel assemblage from the smaller, premound public buildings has the highest percentage of small cooking and serving vessels, suggesting that these structures were used by small groups. In contrast, the emphasis on large vessels in the mound-flank midden and the total absence of small vessels indicates that large-group activities produced that assemblage.

The distribution of functional types and the comparison of orifice diameters suggest that mound-summit activities at Town Creek, at least during the late Town Creek phase, were characterized by food-related activities that involved larger groups of people. Large-scale storage and feasting are two activities that have been associated archaeologically and ethnohistorically with community leaders and public buildings in the Southeast (Blitz 1993a:72, 1993b; Kenton 1927:341, 430–431; McWilliams 1988:88; O'Neill 1977:244; Taft 1996:56–57). The large jars could have been used for communal storage, but the high proportion of larger bowls indicates that food consumption was an important part of these activities. Also, the functional analysis indicates that most larger jars were sooted and thermally altered (Boudreaux 2005:Table 6.2), indicating that they were used for cooking. Therefore, it seems likely that the mound-flank assemblage represents the remains of feasting. Ethnographically, large-scale meals, or feasts, can take a number of forms and serve a variety of purposes (Hayden 2001). They can emphasize social cohesion by establishing and maintaining social ties (Hayden 2001:29; Knight 2001:328). They can also be used as venues for establishing and perpetuating social inequality (Hayden 2001:35; VanDerwarker 1999:24). Among native Southeastern groups, the gathering of community members for feasts was an important and regular part of social and ritual life (Swanton 1979:264; Waselkov and Braund 1995:125). The best-known example of feasting is the communal feast that occurred as part of the annual world renewal rite known as the Green Corn ceremony, an event that did not perpetuate social inequality (Hudson 1976:365; Knight 2001:328).

If feasting took place on the mound summit at Town Creek, it could have been a communal event that fostered social cohesion, a sponsored event that promoted the interests of an individual or particular group such as a lineage, or some combination of the two. Among Historic Southeastern Native societies, group identity was strongly tied to the community's public building or townhouse (DePratter 1983:63; Rodning 2002:10), and a feast located in an analogous context at Town Creek—such as in the public space on the mound summit—also could have been associated with maintaining relationships within the community (see Blitz 1993a:184). The alternative, or perhaps complementary, use of the mound summit at Town Creek for an event that was sponsored by an individual or group would be consistent with a situation in which new political roles were being negotiated. A common way worldwide for leaders to attract and maintain a following in contexts where political roles are not institutionalized is by sponsoring feasts in public places (Dietler 2001:66; Hayden 2001; Kantner 1996:60; Whalen and Minnis 2000:177).

Whether the events that took place on the mound were communal, sponsored, or some combination of the two, the vessel analysis indicates that the place where community-wide political decision-making took place was accessible after mound construction. The vessels from the mound are distinctive from domestic assemblages at Town Creek, suggesting that a dwelling was not located in the mound area either before or after mound construction. Therefore, there does not appear to have been an exclusive association between the mound at Town Creek and a particular family group. Although there certainly were social and political distinctions among individuals and kin groups in the community at all times at Town Creek, mound-summit activities suggest that there was not an exclusive association between these distinctions and public architecture. Instead, the vessel assemblage suggests that the mound summit was a place for large-group gatherings. This finding runs counter to the earthlodge-to-mound model, which proposes that platform mounds as the loci of political decision-making became less accessible (Anderson 1994:120, 1999:220; DePratter 1983:207–208; Wesson 1998:109).

6

Conclusions

This book has attempted to incorporate a wide range of data from as many contexts as possible into an exploration of the relationship between changes in public architecture and changes in social and political roles within the Mississippian community at Town Creek. Along the way, an attempt has been made to sketch out a history of the native community that existed there between roughly A.D. 800 and 1700. Architectural, mortuary, and ceramic data have been incorporated in order to take as broad an approach as possible. However, the research presented here only begins to tap into the potential of the archaeological collections from Town Creek because there are entire artifact classes—such as stone tools, ethnobotanical remains, and faunal remains—that were not incorporated into this research. Also, the potential to test the interpretations presented here through new data collected at Town Creek is virtually limitless because many of the features that were documented at the site have been preserved for future research. Whoever does fieldwork at Town Creek next will have the luxury of knowing where a number of unexcavated structures are located.

Town Creek is important, both to the history of archaeology and to the study of native groups in the Southeast. Joffre Coe's initial work and his vision for long-term research at the site set a course that profoundly affected the direction of the Research Laboratories of Archaeology at the University of North Carolina, the development of a number of archaeologists who went on to careers in the Southeast and beyond, and North Carolina archaeology as a whole. Coe's legacy as well as that of all the people who ever worked at Town Creek—from the field directors to the now anonymous WPA laborers—endures to this day as Town Creek Indian Mound State Historic Site. This legacy also endures in the important research collection, generated by decades of fieldwork, which will be a significant resource for the investigation of Native American lifeways for generations to come.

SUMMARY OF TOWN CREEK'S COMMUNITY HISTORY

Town Creek clearly was an important place in the Pee Dee River Valley for thousands of years. Stone tools indicate that the site was first occupied during the Early Archaic period (8000–6000 B.C. (Coe 1995:Table 10.1), and European trade goods indicate a Native American presence at the site, at least intermittently, through the Protohistoric Caraway phase (A.D. 1500–1700). It is possible that during the Late Woodland period Town Creek was a small, largely vacant ceremonial center that was used intermittently for mortuary ritual by a group that lived in the vicinity or within a territory that included the site. More prominent archaeological signatures at Town Creek during the Late Woodland period indicate that activities at this time were more intense and of a longer duration than previously in the site's history. A Late Woodland structure at Town Creek may have been covered with a low mound similar to those found in the Late Woodland and Early Mississippian burial-mound tradition in the Sandhills region just to the east of the site (Irwin et al. 1999; Ward and Davis 1999:206–210). As increases in population and sedentism possibly led to a "filling" of the landscape in some parts of the Southeast at this time, there may have been an increasing association between groups of people and particular territories (Muller 1997:136–137). Some of the ways a group could have marked its territory include the construction of monuments and the interment of burials, both of which would have provided tangible, immutable evidence of affiliation and ownership (Charles and Buikstra 1983:117; Schroedl and Boyd 1991:83). If the Late Woodland structure at Town Creek had been covered after its destruction by a mound, this monument may have served as a marker of tenure for a group of people living in the vicinity. The act of interring individuals within the Late Woodland structure and essentially turning it into a cemetery could have been a statement about the strength of the group's ties to Town Creek and its vicinity.

The amount of time between the Late Woodland and early Town Creek phase components is unknown, as is the nature of the activities that took place at Town Creek during this interval. Town Creek may have been occupied during the Teal phase (A.D. 900–1050). There are several unexcavated or partially excavated architectural elements in the northern part of the site, including palisade lines in the plaza, that probably predate the early Town Creek phase. The Late Woodland building at Town Creek appears to have been incorporated into the design of the early Town Creek phase community, suggesting that there was not much of a time difference between the building's use and the founding of the Mississippian town. The fact that the Late Woodland and Mississippian occupations both include circular enclosures in which burials were placed suggests continuity between the populations. This contrasts with

Coe's (1952:308) initial view of Town Creek's Pee Dee occupation as a cultural intrusion reflecting the migration of people from the Coast into the Piedmont. Although cultural continuity versus cultural intrusion (see Blitz and Lorenz 2002) has not been directly tested at Town Creek, the apparent continuity between the Late Woodland and early Town Creek phase occupations of Town Creek would be consistent with the latter developing from the former.

The major Mississippian occupation of Town Creek began with the establishment of a town during the early Town Creek phase (A.D. 1050–1250). This settlement consisted of a number of circular houses surrounding the north, south, and east sides of a plaza. The plaza itself contained a large circular enclosure possibly with large posts and a small structure near its center. The entire settlement was surrounded by a palisade that was probably rebuilt several times during the Town Creek phase.

A series of superimposed, rectangular, public buildings representing at least three construction episodes was located on the west side of the plaza. At least two and perhaps all three of these episodes consisted of a larger rectangular building and a smaller square building. The final set of premound public buildings at Town Creek consisted of a small, square, earth-embanked structure to the west, away from the plaza, joined by an entrance trench to a large rectangular, lightly constructed structure to the east adjacent to the plaza. Two of the three smaller square submound buildings at Town Creek were clearly earth-embanked. These two structures are similar to public buildings found across the Southeast during the Etowah (A.D. 1000–1200) and Savannah (A.D. 1200–1350) periods. These earthlodges represent the earliest public architecture at many of these sites, and, as also was the case at Town Creek, many of them were subsequently covered by a platform mound (Crouch 1974; Ferguson 1971:192–193; Rudolph 1984:33–34).

The construction of an earth-embanked structure across from the mound on the eastern side of the plaza at the end of the early Town Creek phase established a public axis that was maintained throughout subsequent occupations. This axis bisected the site along a southwest-northeast line. Public architecture (i.e., the submound public buildings, circular enclosure, large postholes, and earth-embanked structure next to the river) was placed on and sometimes oriented to this axis, while houses were located to the north and south of this line.

A significant change occurred within the sphere of public architecture during the late Town Creek phase (A.D. 1250–1300) with the construction of a platform mound approximately 5 ft in height on the western end of the plaza. There was a clear continuity between the premound public buildings and the mound, though, because the former covered the latter and they shared the same orientation. Although the first mound summit was not reached by excavations, it is likely—based on the premound buildings, those on subsequent mound summits, and those at other South Appalachian sites (Polhemus 1987; Smith 1994)—that the structures located on the late Town Creek phase mound summit consisted of one or two small, square, earth-embanked buildings on the west side of the summit and a large, rectangular, more ephemeral building located on the east side. Two mound stages were added during the Leak phase, but they were much smaller than the initial episode of mound construction. Each Leak phase mound stage contained an identical arrangement of two small, square structures joined by an entrance trench on the west side of the summit. Although the eastern part of the summit was not present because it had been destroyed by looters, it probably contained a large, open, rectangular structure. Each of the structures that was present had been burned (Coe 1995:81–82), perhaps as part of a ritual destruction intended for public spectacle (see Creel and Anyon 2003:77).

The public axis established during the early Town Creek phase was maintained after mound construction. The large, circular enclosure in the plaza was removed at some point during the Town Creek phase, although it is possible that one or more of the large posts in the plaza remained. A large, rectangular enclosure that surrounded a square structure and two burial clusters was built on the public axis on the eastern side of the plaza adjacent to the riverbank. This enclosure appears to have been oriented relative to two burials that were aligned with features of premound public buildings across the plaza. While the activities performed within the rectangular enclosure are unknown, it clearly was a special location and denotes an intent to demarcate and possibly restrict access to this part of the site. There are clear connections between the mound and the rectangular enclosure. Both are oriented in the same way and are located along the site's public axis. In addition, the most unusual artifacts in the postmound-construction community were associated with burials in these two contexts. It is possible that the rectangular enclosure was a mortuary facility associated with the mound. A relationship between mound-summit buildings and mortuary structures has been documented both ethnohistorically (O'Neill 1977:240) and archaeologically (Blitz 1993a:96; Knight 1998:52; Schnell et al. 1981:Figures 2.3 and 2.6) at other Mississippian sites.

New structure types appeared after mound construction during the late Town Creek phase on the north and south sides of the plaza. One type was a large rectangular structure that contained a few well-spaced burials across its interior. The other was a large circular enclosure that surrounded a densely packed cemetery with a large number of burials. Structures of these two types do not overlap, and they appear to alternate around the edge of the plaza, suggesting that adjacent structures of each type may have been paired together to form a functional unit. It appears that at least four such pairs existed at Town Creek, although patterns are less clear in unexcavated portions of the site.

The fact that the rectangular structures and enclosed cemeteries were located in the domestic portion of the site suggests that they were used by the same kin groups or lineages that had occupied this area during the early Town Creek phase. It is likely that at least some, and possibly all, of the enclosed cemeteries used during the late Town Creek–Leak phases actually began as the locations of houses during the early Town Creek phase. The maintenance of house sites for long periods of time has been recognized in other Mississippian communities, and the perpetuation of former house sites as enclosed cemeteries at Town Creek may represent "the physical expression of an ideological emphasis on household identity and continuity through time" (Hally and Kelly 1998:61). Although the structures to the north and south of the plaza may have been used by kin-based groups that had previously lived in these locations, there is no evidence for clearly domestic architecture in any of the excavated portions of Town Creek following mound construction. Instead, it seems that ancestral house sites were preserved by kin groups through the maintenance of an enclosed cemetery and through the construction of an adjacent rectangular structure that, based on its size, may have served as a meeting place for the kin group. Mortuary data suggest that burial within the enclosed cemeteries was open to all members of the kin group. while burial in the rectangular structures was restricted to a subset of the group.

At the large Mississippian site of Moundville in Alabama, pairs of mounds have been interpreted as having supported a mortuary temple and a public building that was an elite residence associated with a particular corporate group (Knight 1998:51–54). These mound pairs are seen as the modular units that collectively constitute Moundville's impressive configuration of platform mounds (Knight 1998:52). It is plausible that a similar situation existed at Town Creek during the late Town Creek–Leak phases (A.D. 1250–1350) with the plaza being surrounded by pairs of structures—consisting of a mortuary facility and a public building—that were associated with individual corporate groups.

Moundville and Town Creek represent opposite ends of the Mississippian spectrum in many ways, including site size, number of mounds, amount of nonlocal exchange, and degree of social differentiation (Knight and Steponaitis 1998; Peebles 1971; Peebles and Kus 1977; Welch 1991). Regardless of these important differences, the two sites are similar in that they were occupied for very long periods of time, and both shifted from being more domestic to more ceremonial in function later in their occupations (Knight and Steponaitis 1998:18–19; Steponaitis 1998). Interestingly, the preeminent Mississippian site of Cahokia in Illinois also experienced a significant decrease in population late in its occupation (Knight 1997:239–241; Pauketat 1994:186). An increased disparity in status between leaders and the rest of the community is one possible explanation for the movement of people out of these large Mississippian towns. As Mississippian leaders at Cahokia and Moundville became more sanctified through time, they either dispersed households to distance themselves from the populace, or community members chose to leave these towns in order to avoid the ceremonial, economic, or social burdens that may have come with living in close proximity to their leaders (Knight 1997:238–240; Knight and Steponaitis 1998:19; Pauketat 1994:186; Steponaitis 1978:448). At Town Creek, where social differences—and presumably obligations—appear to have been less pronounced, the reasons for the changes in architecture to the north and south of the plaza are unclear. The absence of domestic architecture during the late Town Creek–Leak phases suggests that residents of the Town Creek community were dispersed at that time beyond the bounds of the original settlement. At present, the degree of population dispersal is unknown. People could have moved well away from Town Creek and been living in settlements in the surrounding area, or they could have been living just beyond the limits of excavations only tens of feet from the plaza. If populations were more scattered during the late Town Creek–Leak phases, then the rectangular structures and enclosed cemeteries located along the plaza may have been the loci of rituals and gatherings that served the purpose of maintaining ties within these more dispersed groups.

The character of Town Creek following mound construction appears to have shifted from the presence of houses around the whole site and relatively large-scale mound construction to much smaller mound stages and the absence of any clearly domestic structures. If population decreased at Town Creek following the appearance of the mound, then the decreased level of mound construction that occurred may have been correlated with the declining size of the resident population. Most of the mound was built during the transition from early Town Creek to late Town Creek phase (ca. A.D. 1250) when multiple houses were occupied, while much smaller construction stages were added during the Leak phase when the resident population may have been much smaller. The relationship between the large rectangular structures and enclosed cemeteries around the plaza may have been that the former were places where corporate groups met for integrative events while the latter were kin-based cemeteries. Town Creek has been interpreted in the past as a vacant ceremonial center devoted primarily to mortuary ritual (Coe 1995:264–268; Oliver 1992:60), an interpretation that many, myself included, have seen as inconsistent with the evidence (Ward and Davis 1999:133). While this interpretation does not fit with the early Town Creek phase data, the view of Town

Creek as a ceremonial center may not be far from the mark for at least one part of its Mississippian occupation—the late Town Creek–Leak phases.

The plazas of both Moundville and Town Creek were surrounded by the public buildings of the corporate groups that constituted each community. The most obvious difference between the two sites is that the corporate-group buildings at Moundville were elevated on platform mounds (Knight 1998) while those at Town Creek were not. The size and arrangement of the mounds at Moundville appear to be physical manifestations of the social and political relationships that existed among and within the corporate groups that constituted the Mississippian community there (Knight 1998). The Moundville site was planned and initially constructed at a time of significant regional political competition (Knight and Steponaitis 1998:17). According to Knight (1998:59–60), emerging leaders used mound construction within the context of existing kinship/corporate-group relationships as an arena for political competition. While Town Creek and Moundville are similar in that both appear to have had corporate-group public buildings located around their plazas, the fact that Town Creek had only one mound—a mound that was not exclusively associated with a particular family—may reflect the degree of political competition within the Mississippian community there. It is interesting that each community followed a similar trajectory from domestic to ceremonial in nature and shared the site-structure components of having preeminent public buildings located on a central axis with corporate-group public buildings surrounding a plaza. Emergent political leaders at Moundville competed within the existing kinship structure by incorporating their residences into corporate-group, mound-summit buildings (Knight 1998:60). While corporate-group public buildings were built around the plaza at Town Creek as well, a key difference is that public buildings do not appear to have also served as residences, indicating that at Town Creek there was not an exclusive link between an individual or a particular family and a public building. Knight (1998:60) argues that the spatial arrangement of mounds at Moundville, primarily the construction of a massive mound that was the residence of a leader on the site's central axis, reflects the ability of leaders to transcend the traditional kinship structure and assume the role of a paramount chief. While corporate groups and their public buildings also were the fundamental components of the community at Town Creek, it seems that the absence of intense economic, political, and social competition did not lead to the exclusive association of public buildings with particular leaders.

Town Creek appears to have had a robust Mississippian occupation during the thirteenth and fourteenth centuries but likely was abandoned some time during the fifteenth century. This chronology fits with a broader pattern of population reorganization and movement in the Southeast at about A.D. 1450, when many sites, including those in the central and lower Savannah River Valley, were abandoned (Anderson 1994:326). Such regional-scale abandonment may correlate with prolonged periods of drought that would have undermined the maize-based political and subsistence economies of local Mississippian societies (Anderson 1994:327; Anderson et al. 1995). It is possible that Town Creek was affected by the same conditions.

LEADERSHIP AND MOUND CONSTRUCTION AT TOWN CREEK

An important assumption underlying many interpretations of Mississippian societies is that the presence of a mound signifies major differences in population dynamics as well as social and political organization (Anderson 1994:80; Hally 1999; Holley 1999:33–35; Lewis and Stout 1998:231–232; Lindauer and Blitz 1997; Milner and Schroeder 1999:96; Muller 1997:275–276; Steponaitis 1978, 1986:389–392). The architectural and mortuary patterns from Town Creek indicate that changes were associated with mound construction. The mound appears at or about the same time that corporate-group public buildings replaced houses around the plaza. Mortuary data indicate that there were some changes in the nature of leadership between the premound-construction and postmound-construction communities at Town Creek. The differences in the composition of the burial populations between premound and postmound public buildings, with an emphasis on older and mature adults in the former and young adults in the latter, coupled with the presence of new artifact types, suggest that the people buried in public spaces following mound construction occupied new social and political roles. An early Town Creek phase political organization that was more diffuse and representative and that could still be seen as equal to or less important than family and household ties was replaced after mound construction by a form of social and political organization in which some individuals—primarily young adults—were clearly distinct and their ties to a community-wide status, which seems to have been closely related to ritual activities, were more important than their ties to family and household.

While there are clear differences between the premound and postmound communities at Town Creek, they do not necessarily fit with the expectation that mounds signify hierarchical social and economic relationships. Making a distinction between "elites" and "non-elites" has become an important part of how we investigate Mississippian societies (see Maxham 2000:337–338; Muller 1997:47–50: Steponaitis 1986:389–390). There are a number of cases in the ethnohistoric literature (Butler 1934; Clayton et al. 1993; Kenton 1927;

McWilliams 1988; O'Neill 1977) and archaeological record (Brown 1971:101; Fowler et al. 1999:187–188; Knight and Steponaitis 1998:18; Peebles and Kus 1977:439) of native Southeastern societies in which there seem to be clear hierarchical social distinctions between different groups of people. At Town Creek, such stark distinctions are absent from the archaeological record. Instead, political power within the Mississippian community at Town Creek seems to have been heterarchical in nature and was likely shared by multiple social groups both before and after mound construction. Older adults, adult women, and lineage leaders may have participated in the political decision-making process prior to mound construction. Although the burial treatments of some individuals were more distinctive following mound construction, the representation of multiple social groups in prominent locations within the community suggests that its political structure was still heterarchical. The people buried in the mound, the rectangular enclosure, the kin-group cemeteries, and the kin-group public buildings may all represent distinctive social groups that participated in the political process following mound construction. The differences that are manifested among individuals following mound construction are subtle and relative, although they were surely important to the residents of the Town Creek community. Some people were "elite" in a relative sense in that they were afforded burial in public places, were associated with unusual artifacts, and played important roles in community rituals. There is no evidence, though, that these same people lived substantially different lives than anyone else in the community (see Milner 1998:160; Muller 1997:47–48). This view is consistent with numerous ethnohistoric observations of egalitarian village societies in which community leaders were recognized as such and were treated with a certain amount of deference in particular contexts (e.g., council meetings), but that they were treated normally outside of these contexts and were largely indistinguishable from other community members in dress and possessions (Moore 1988:32, 33, 44, 64; Waselkov and Braund 1995:117, 118, 147; Williams 1930:459–460).

A consistently cited expression of political power in Mississippian societies is the ability of leaders to place their residence on the summit of a platform mound (Brown 1997:475; Milanich et al. 1997:118; Steponaitis 1986:386) with the clear statement that this person was now associated with a symbol of group identity (Knight 1989b:287) and the locus of political authority (Hally 1996, 1999; Knight 1998:60). Ethnohistoric accounts of the Natchez indicate that the chief was identified with the mound on which he lived and that both were treated with the same respect, fear, and deference (Kenton 1927:341, 431). If the mound summit at Town Creek was the location of the community leader's residence, then the construction of the platform mound over earlier public buildings could be interpreted as a statement about increasing political authority—as proposed in the earthlodge-to-platform mound model (Anderson 1994:119–120, 1999:220; DePratter 1983:207–208; Rudolph 1984:40). There is little evidence for the increased centralization of political authority at Town Creek, however, if the leader's residence was not located on the mound but was instead among other domestic structures, as was the case during the early Town Creek phase before the mound was built.

Although it is generally accepted that many mounds were the loci of elite residences (Holley 1999:28; Lewis et al. 1998:17; Payne 1994:155; Steponaitis 1986:390), mound functions were variable (see Blitz 1999:583; Knight 2004: 318–319; Lindauer and Blitz 1997:175–176). One reason to think that the buildings on the mound summit at Town Creek were not domestic is that the burial populations associated with them are demographically restricted, unlike the more representative populations associated with the circular structures and enclosed cemeteries around the plaza that were likely associated with households and kin-based groups. Another indication that the summit buildings were not domestic is that their configuration was likely similar to those of the public buildings that immediately preceded mound construction, all of which were clearly distinct in several ways from contemporaneous domestic structures. The last set of premound public buildings at Town Creek consisted of a large, relatively open area for the gathering of large groups and an adjacent, more restricted structure accessible only to a subset of the community. The vessel data from the mound summit are not consistent with the idea that a residence was located there or that the summit—as the locus of community political authority—was less accessible. Instead, the vessel data suggest that the mound summit was the site of feasting, and the target audience was large groups of people. Collectively, the components of the submound and mound-summit public buildings at Town Creek do not resemble houses but are instead reminiscent of historically documented sets of public buildings in the Southeast that consisted of a large pavilion used for public meetings that involved feasting and an enclosed building to which access was limited (Waselkov and Braund 1995:104–105, Figures 21 and 22).

The inference that mound construction can be equated with political centralization is based on the idea that a residence was placed on a mound that had covered an earlier form of public architecture in which political decisions were made through consensus. If the rectilinear public buildings located on the west side of the plaza at Town Creek began as nonresidential public buildings and continued as such at least through the Leak phase, then the premise of the earthlodge-to-platform-mound model from which political centralization is inferred is not applicable at Town Creek. While one should not argue that the earthlodge-to-platform-mound transition at other sites occurred in exactly the same way, the patterns at Town Creek raise the question of at how many other Mississippian mound sites is the model not applicable.

Town Creek is a relatively small mound site located on the periphery of the Mississippian world. As such, the findings presented here on social differences and community development could be dismissed as being of limited utility for more "typical" Mississippian sites. I argue, however, that the subtle manifestations of social and political differences at Town Creek are important to current Mississippian studies. When the entire Mississippian world is considered, there are few clear cases of hierarchical social differences that were also imbued with differences in wealth and power, and there is little evidence to support the idea that such relationships were typical (see Milner 1998:162–163; Muller 1997:396–399). This is not to say that social differences did not exist, because they clearly did. Indeed, the mortuary patterns at Town Creek are consistent with the idea that some people occupied distinctive social and political statuses. However, the patterns at Town Creek may, in fact, be more typical of the overwhelming majority of Mississippian mound sites that are exactly like Town Creek, relatively small with a single platform mound (Blitz and Livingood 2004:Figure 7; Payne 1994:80). Unless one assumes that all of these single-mound sites were embedded within the settlement system of a complex chiefdom, an interpretation that has been called into question (see Blitz 1999), then the patterns at Town Creek are likely more reflective of those that existed within a "typical" Mississippian society than are the truly exceptional manifestations of social differences documented archaeologically at Cahokia and Moundville and ethnohistorically among the Natchez.

References

Adler, Michael A., and Richard H. Wilshusen
  1990   Large-scale Integrative Facilities in Tribal Societies: Cross-cultural and South-western U.S. Examples. *World Archaeology* 22(2):133–146.
Anderson, David G.
  1982   *The Mattassee Lake Sites: Archeological Investigations along the Lower Santee River in the Coastal Plain of South Carolina.* Commonwealth Associates Inc. Submitted to United States Department of the Interior, Contract Number C54030(80). National Park Service, Interagency Archeological Services, Atlanta.
  1989   The Mississippian in South Carolina. In *Studies in South Carolina Archaeology: Essays in Honor of Robert L. Stephenson,* edited by Albert C. Goodyear III and Glen T. Hanson, pp. 101–131. Anthropological Studies 9, Occasional Papers of the South Carolina Institute of Archaeology and Anthropology, University of South Carolina, Columbia.
  1994   *The Savannah River Chiefdoms: Political Change in the Late Prehistoric Southeast.* University of Alabama Press, Tuscaloosa.
  1999   Examining Chiefdoms in the Southeast: An Application of Multiscalar Analysis. In *Great Towns and Regional Polities in the Prehistoric American Southwest and Southeast,* edited by Jill E. Neitzel, pp. 215–241. University of New Mexico Press, Albuquerque.
Anderson, David G., David J. Hally, and James L. Rudolph
  1986   The Mississippian Occupation of the Savannah River Valley. *Southeastern Archaeology* 5(1):32–51.
Anderson, David G., David W. Stahle, and Malcolm K. Cleaveland
  1995   Paleoclimate and the Potential Food Reserves of Mississippian Societies: A Case Study from the Savannah River Valley. *American Antiquity* 60(2):258–286.
Bennett, Leslie J.
  1984   A Mortuary Analysis of Early Mississippian Status Structure along the Tombigbee River. Unpublished Master's thesis, Department of Anthropology, State University of New York, Binghamton.
Binford, Lewis R.
  1971   Mortuary Practices: Their Study and Their Potential. In *Approaches to the Social Dimensions of Mortuary Practices,* edited by James A. Brown, pp. 6–27. Number 25. Memoirs of the Society for American Archaeology, Washington, D.C.

Blanton, Richard E., Gary M. Feinman, Stephen A. Kowalewski, and Peter N. Peregrine
1996   A Dual-Processual Theory of the Evolution of Mesoamerican Civilization. *Current Anthropology* 37(1):1–14.

Blitz, John H.
1993a   *Ancient Chiefdoms of the Tombigbee.* University of Alabama Press, Tuscaloosa.
1993b   Big Pots for Big Shots: Feasting and Storage in a Mississippian Community. *American Antiquity* 58(1):80–96.
1999   Mississippian Chiefdoms and the Fission-Fusion Process. *American Antiquity* 64(4):577–592.

Blitz, John H., and Patrick Livingood
2004   Sociopolitical Implications of Mississippian Mound Volume. *American Antiquity* 69(2):291–301.

Blitz, John H., and Karl G. Lorenz
2002   The Early Mississippian Frontier in the Lower Chattahoochee–Apalachicola River Valley. In *Frontiers, Backwaters, and Peripheries: Exploring the Edges of the Mississippian World,* edited by Adam King and Maureen S. Meyers, special thematic section *Southeastern Archaeology* 21(2):117–135.

Boudreaux, Edmond A.
2005   The Archaeology of Town Creek: Chronology, Community Patterns, and Leadership at a Mississippian Town. Unpublished Ph.D. dissertation, Department of Anthropology, University of North Carolina, Chapel Hill.

Boudreaux, Edmond A., and R. P. Stephen Davis, Jr.
2002   The Town Creek Photographic Mosaic: Old Pictures in a New Light. Poster Presented at the 59th Annual Meeting of the Southeastern Archaeological Conference, Biloxi, Mississippi.

Brain, Jeffrey P.
1979   *Tunica Treasure.* Papers of the Peabody Museum of Archaeology and Ethnology Volume 71, Harvard University, Cambridge, Massachusetts.

Brain, Jeffrey P., and Philip Phillips
1996   *Shell Gorgets: Styles of the Late Prehistoric and Protohistoric Southeast.* Peabody Museum Press, Cambridge, Massachusetts.

Braun, David P.
1980   Appendix I: Experimental Interpretation of Ceramic Vessel Use on the Basis of Rim and Neck Formal Attributes. In *The Navajo Project: Archaeological Investigations, Page to Phoenix 500 KV Southern Transmission Line,* by Donald C. Fiero, Robert W. Munson, Martha T. McClain, Suzanne M. Wilson, and Anne H. Zier, pp. 171–231. Research Paper 11. Museum of Northern Arizona, Flagstaff.

Braund, Kathryn E. Holland (editor)
1999   *A Concise Natural History of East and West Florida,* by Bernard Romans. Univer-
[1775] sity of Alabama Press, Tuscaloosa.

Brown, James A.
1971   Dimensions of Status in the Burials at Spiro. In *Approaches to the Social Dimensions of Mortuary Practices,* edited by James A. Brown, pp. 92–112. Number 25. Memoirs of the Society for American Archaeology, Washington, D.C.
1997   The Archaeology of Ancient Religion in the Eastern Woodlands. *Annual Review of Anthropology* 26:465–485.

Butler, Ruth Lapham (translator)
1934   *Journal of Paul Du Ru [February 1 to May 8, 1700]: Missionary Priest to Loui-siana.* The Caxton Club, Chicago.

Cable, John
2000a Demographic Succession as a Factor in Explaining Offsetting Occupation Spans at Mississippian Mound Centers. Paper presented at the 57th Annual Meeting of the Southeastern Archaeological Conference, Macon, Georgia.
2000b Late Woodland and Etowah Occupations. In *Archaeological Excavations in Brass-town Valley,* special thematic issue of *Early Georgia* 28(2):102–111.

Caldwell, Joseph R.
1958   *Trend and Tradition in the Prehistory of the Eastern United States.* Memoir Number 88. American Anthropological Association, Springfield, Illinois.

Carneiro, Robert L.
1981   The Chiefdom: Precursor to the State. In *The Transition to Statehood in the New World,* edited by Grant D. Jones and Robert R. Kautz, pp. 37–79. Cambridge University Press, Cambridge.

Charles, Douglas K., and Jane E. Buikstra
1983   Archaic Mortuary Sites in the Central Mississippi Drainage: Distribution, Structure, and Behavioral Implications. In *Archaic Hunters and Gatherers in the American Midwest,* edited by James L. Phillips and James A. Brown, pp. 117–144. Academic Press, New York.

Claassen, Cheryl
2001   Challenges for Regendering Southeastern Prehistory. In *Archaeological Stud-ies of Gender in the Southeastern United States,* edited by Jane M. Eastman and Christopher B. Rodning, pp. 10–26. University Press of Florida, Gaines-ville.

Clayton, Lawrence A., Vernon J. Knight, Jr., and Edward C. Moore (editors)
1993   *The De Soto Chronicles: The Expedition of Hernando de Soto to North America in 1539–1543.* University of Alabama Press, Tuscaloosa.

Cobb, Charles R.
1989   An Appraisal of the Role of Mill Creek Chert Hoes in Mississippian Exchange Systems. *Southeastern Archaeology* 8(2):79–92.
2000   *From Quarry to Cornfield: The Political Economy of Mississippian Hoe Produc-tion.* University of Alabama Press, Tuscaloosa.

Coe, Joffre L.
1937 Mg^02 Frutchey Mound Horizontal Profile. Map on file, Research Laboratories of Archaeology, University of North Carolina, Chapel Hill.
1940   *Quarterly Report of the WPA-UNC Archaeological Project.* Occasional Contribu-tions Number 1. Laboratory of Anthropology and Archaeology, University of North Carolina, Chapel Hill.
1952   The Cultural Sequence of the Carolina Piedmont. In *Archeology of Eastern United States,* edited by James B. Griffin, pp. 301–311. University of Chicago Press, Chicago.
1964   The Formative Cultures of the Carolina Piedmont. *Transactions of the American Philosophical Society* Volume 54, Part 5. Philadelphia.
1995   *Town Creek Indian Mound: A Native American Legacy.* University of North Carolina Press, Chapel Hill.

Creel, Darrell, and Roger Anyon
2003   New Interpretations of Mimbres Public Architecture and Space: Implications for Cultural Change. *American Antiquity* 68(1):67–92.

Crouch, Daniel J.
1974   South Appalachian Earth Lodges. Unpublished Master's thesis, Department of Anthropology, University of North Carolina, Chapel Hill.

Crumley, Carole L.
1987   A Dialectical Critique of Hierarchy. In *Power Relations and State Formation*, edited by Thomas C. Patterson and Christine W. Gailey, pp. 155–169. American Anthropological Association, Washington, D.C.
1995   Introduction. In *Heterarchy and the Analysis of Complex Societies*, edited by Robert M. Ehrenreich, Carole L. Crumley, and Janet E. Levy, pp. 1–5. Number 6. Archeological Papers of the American Anthropological Association, Washington, D.C.

Culin, Stewart
1975   *Games of the North American Indians*. Reprinted. Dover Publications Inc., New York. Originally published 1907, Annual Report 24, Bureau of American Ethnology, United States Government Printing Office, Washington, D.C.

Davis, R. P. Stephen, Jr., Patricia M. Lambert, Vincas P. Steponaitis, Clark Spence Larsen, and H. Trawick Ward
1996   *NAGPRA Inventory of Human Remains and Funerary Objects from Town Creek Indian Mound*. Research Laboratories of Anthropology, University of North Carolina, Chapel Hill.

Deagan, Kathleen
1987   *Artifacts of the Spanish Colonies of Florida and the Caribbean, 1500–1800*, Volume 1, *Ceramics, Glassware, and Beads*. Smithsonian Institution Press, Washington.

Demel, Scott J., and Robert L. Hall
1998   The Mississippian Town Plan and Cultural Landscape of Cahokia, Illinois. In *Mississippian Towns and Sacred Spaces: Searching for an Architectural Grammar*, edited by R. Barry Lewis and Charles Stout, pp. 200–226. University of Alabama Press, Tuscaloosa.

DePratter, Chester B.
1983   *Late Prehistoric and Early Historic Chiefdoms in the Southeastern United States*. Ph.D. dissertation, University of Georgia, Athens. University Microfilms, Ann Arbor.

DePratter, Chester B., and Christopher Judge
1990   Wateree River. In *Lamar Archaeology: Mississippian Chiefdoms in the Deep South*, edited by Mark Williams and Gary Shapiro, pp. 56–58. University of Alabama Press, Tuscaloosa.

Dickens, Roy S., Jr.
1968   The Construction of a Photographic Mosaic for the Town Creek Archaeological Site, Montgomery County, North Carolina. Manuscript on file, Research Laboratories of Archaeology, Chapel Hill.

Dietler, Michael
2001   Theorizing the Feast: Rituals of Consumption, Commensal Politics, and Power in African Contexts. In *Feasts: Archaeological and Ethnographic Perspectives on*

Food, Politics, and Power, edited by Michael Dietler and Brian Hayden, pp. 65–114. Smithsonian Institution Press, Washington, D.C.

Dillehay, Tom D.
1990   Mapuche Ceremonial Landscape, Social Recruitment and Resource Rights. *World Archaeology* 22(2):223–241.

Driscoll, Elizabeth Monahan
2001   Bioarchaeology, Mortuary Patterning, and Social Organization at Town Creek. Unpublished Ph.D. dissertation, Department of Anthropology, University of North Carolina, Chapel Hill.
2002   Mortuary Patterning and Social Organization at Town Creek Mound and Village. In *The Archaeology of Native North Carolina: Papers in Honor of H. Trawick Ward,* edited by Jane M. Eastman, Christopher B. Rodning, and Edmond A. Boudreaux III, pp. 18–27. Special Publication 7, Southeastern Archaeological Conference, Biloxi, Mississippi.

Dye, David H.
2000   The Accoutrements of High Office: Elite Ritual Paraphernalia from Pickwick Basin. Paper presented at the 57th Annual Meeting of the Southeastern Archaeological Conference, Macon, Georgia.

Earle, Timothy
1989   The Evolution of Chiefdoms. *Current Anthropology* 30(1):84–88.
1991   The Evolution of Chiefdoms. In *Chiefdoms: Power, Economy, and Ideology,* edited by Timothy Earle, pp. 1–15. Cambridge University Press, Cambridge.
1997   *How Chiefs Come to Power: The Political Economy in Prehistory.* Stanford University Press, Stanford.

Eastman, Jane M.
1994   The North Carolina Radiocarbon Date Study (Part 1). *Southern Indian Studies* 42:1–63.
2001   Life Courses and Gender among Late Prehistoric Siouan Communities. In *Archaeological Studies of Gender in the Southeastern United States,* edited by Jane M. Eastman and Christopher B. Rodning, pp. 57–76. University Press of Florida, Gainesville.

Eastman, Jane M., and Christopher B. Rodning (editors)
2001   *Archaeological Studies of Gender in the Southeastern United States.* University Press of Florida, Gainesville.

Emerson, Thomas E.
1997   *Cahokia and the Archaeology of Power.* University of Alabama Press, Tuscaloosa and London.

Fairbanks, Charles H.
1946   The Macon Earth Lodge. *American Antiquity* 12(2):94–108.

Feinman, Gary, and Jill Neitzel
1984   Too Many Types: An Overview of Sedentary Prestate Societies in the Americas. In *Advances in Archaeological Method and Theory,* Volume 7, edited by Michael B. Schiffer, pp. 39–102. Academic Press, Orlando.

Ferguson, Leland G.
1971   South Appalachian Mississippian. Unpublished Ph.D. dissertation, Department of Anthropology, University of North Carolina, Chapel Hill.
1995   Foreword. In *Town Creek Indian Mound: A Native American Legacy,* by Joffre L. Coe, pp. xiii–xx. University of North Carolina Press, Chapel Hill and London.

Flannery, Kent V.
 1999   Chiefdoms in the Early Near East: Why It's So Hard to Identify Them. In *The Iranian World: Essays on Iranian Art and Archaeology, Presented to Ezat O. Negahban,* edited by Abbas Alizadeh, Yousef Majidzadeh, and Sadeq Malek Shahmirzadi, pp. 44–58. Iran University Press, Tehran.

Fowler, Melvin L., Jerome Rose, Barbara Vander Leest, and Steven R. Ahler
 1999   *The Mound 72 Area: Dedicated and Sacred Space in Early Cahokia.* Reports of Investigations Number 54. Illinois State Museum, Springfield.

Fox, William A.
 2004   The North-South Copper Axis. *Southeastern Archaeology* 23(1):85–97.

Gearing, Fred
 1958   The Structural Poses of 18th Century Cherokee Villages. *American Anthropologist* 60(6):1148–1157.

Griffin, James B.
 1967   Eastern North American Archaeology: A Summary. *Science* 156(3772):175–191.
 1985a Changing Concepts of the Prehistoric Mississippian Cultures of the Eastern United States. In *Alabama and the Borderlands from Prehistory to Statehood,* edited by R. Reid Badger and Lawrence A. Clayton, pp. 40–63. University of Alabama Press, Tuscaloosa.
 1985b Joffre Lanning Coe: The Quiet Giant of Southeastern Archaeology. In *Structure and Process in Southeastern Archaeology,* edited by Roy S. Dickens, Jr., and H. Trawick Ward, pp. 287–304. University of Alabama Press, Tuscaloosa.

Hall, Robert L.
 1996   American Indian Worlds, World Quarters, World Centers, and Their Shrines. *The Wisconsin Archeologist* 77(3/4):120–127.

Hally, David J.
 1983   Use Alteration of Pottery Vessel Surfaces: An Important Source of Evidence for the Identification of Vessel Function. *North American Archaeologist* 4(1):3–26.
 1984   Vessel Assemblages and Food Habits: A Comparison of Two Aboriginal Southeastern Vessel Assemblages. *Southeastern Archaeology* 3(1):46–64.
 1986   The Identification of Vessel Function: A Case Study from Northwest Georgia. *American Antiquity* 51(2):267–295.
 1994   An Overview of Lamar Culture. In *Ocumulgee Archaeology, 1936–1986,* edited by David J. Hally, pp. 144–174. University of Georgia Press, Athens and London.
 1996   Platform-Mound Construction and the Instability of Mississippian Chiefdoms. In *Political Structure and Change in the Prehistoric Southeastern United States,* edited by John F. Scarry, pp. 92–127. University Press of Florida, Gainesville.
 1999   The Settlement Pattern of Mississippian Chiefdoms in Northern Georgia. In *Settlement Pattern Studies in the Americas: Fifty Years since Virú,* edited by Brian R. Billman and Gary M. Feinman, pp. 96–115. Smithsonian Institution Press, Washington and London.
 2002   "As caves below the ground": Making Sense of Aboriginal House Form in the Protohistoric and Historic Southeast. In *Between Contact and Colonies: Archaeological Perspectives on the Protohistoric Southeast,* edited by Cameron B. Wesson and Mark A. Rees, pp. 90–109. University of Alabama Press, Tuscaloosa and London.

Hally, David J., and Hypatia Kelly
 1998   The Nature of Mississippian Towns in Georgia: The King Site Example. In *Mis-*

sissippian Towns and Sacred Spaces: Searching for an Architectural Grammar, edited by R. Barry Lewis and Charles Stout, pp. 49–63. University of Alabama Press, Tuscaloosa and London.

Hally, David J., and James B. Langford, Jr.
1988 *Mississippi Period Archaeology of the Georgia Valley and Ridge Province.* Report Number 25. University of Georgia Laboratory of Archaeology Series, Athens.

Hally, David J., and James L. Rudolph
1986 *Mississippi Period Archaeology of the Georgia Piedmont.* Report Number 24. University of Georgia Laboratory of Archaeology Series, Athens.

Hayden, Brian
2001 Fabulous Feasts: A Prolegomenon to the Importance of Feasting. In *Feasts: Archaeological and Ethnographic Perspectives on Food, Politics, and Power,* edited by Michael Dietler and Brian Hayden, pp. 23–64. Smithsonian Institution Press, Washington and London.

Helms, Mary W.
1979 *Ancient Panama: Chiefs in Search of Power.* University of Texas Press, Austin and London.

Henrickson, Elizabeth F., and Mary M. A. McDonald
1983 Ceramic Form and Function: An Ethnographic Search and an Archeological Application. *American Anthropologist* 85:630–643.

Hodder, Ian
1982 The Identification and Interpretation of Ranking in Prehistory: A Contextual Perspective. In *Ranking, Resource, and Exchange: Aspects of the Archaeology of Early European Society,* edited by Colin Renfrew and Stephen Shennan, pp. 150–154. Cambridge University Press, Cambridge.

Holley, George R.
1999 Late Prehistoric Towns in the Southeast. In *Great Towns and Regional Polities in the Prehistoric American Southwest and Southeast,* edited by Jill E. Neitzel, pp. 22–38. University of New Mexico Press, Albuquerque.

Howell, Todd L.
1995 Tracking Zuni Gender and Leadership Roles across the Contact Period. *Journal of Anthropological Research* 51:125–147.
1996 Identifying Leaders at Hawikku. *Kiva* 62(1):61–82.

Hudson, Charles
1976 *The Southeastern Indians.* University of Tennessee Press, Knoxville.
1990 *The Juan Pardo Expeditions: Exploration of the Carolinas and Tennessee, 1566–1568.* Smithsonian Institution Press, Washington and London.

Irwin, Jeffrey D., Wayne C. J. Boyko, Joseph M. Herbert, and Chad Braley
1999 Woodland Burial Mounds in the North Carolina Sandhills and Southern Coastal Plain. *North Carolina Archaeology* 48:59–86.

Jefferies, Richard W.
1994 The Swift Creek Site and Woodland Platform Mounds in the Southeastern United States. In *Ocmulgee Archaeology, 1936–1986,* edited by David J. Hally, pp. 71–83. University of Georgia Press, Athens and London.

Judge, Christopher
2003 An Overview of the Mississippian Ceramic Sequence for the Wateree River Valley, South Carolina. Paper presented at the Sixtieth Annual Meeting of the Southeastern Archaeological Conference, Charlotte, North Carolina.

Kantner, John
1996   Political Competition among the Chaco Anasazi of the American Southwest. *Journal of Anthropological Archaeology* 15:41–105.

Kelly, A. R.
1974   Excavation History at the Mulberry Plantation. *The Notebook* 6(3–4):67–87.

Kelly, John E.
1990   Range Site Community Patterns and the Mississippian Emergence. In *The Mississippian Emergence*, edited by Bruce D. Smith, pp. 67–112. Smithsonian Institution Press, Washington and London.

Kenton, Edna (editor)
1927   *The Indians of North America: From "The Jesuit Relations and Allied Documents: Travels and Explorations of the Jesuit Missionaries in New France, 1610–1791."* Edited by Reuben Gold Thwaites, Volume 2. Harcourt, Brace, and Company, New York.

Keyes, Greg
1994   Myth and Social History in the Early Southeast. In *Perspectives on the Southeast: Linguistics, Archaeology, and Ethnohistory*, edited by Patricia B. Kwachka, pp. 106–115. University of Georgia Press, Athens and London.

Kidd, Kenneth E., and Martha A. Kidd
1970   A Classification System for Glass Beads for the Use of Field Archaeologists. *Canadian Historic Sites, Occasional Papers in Archaeology and History* 1:46–89.

King, Adam
2003   *Etowah: The Political History of a Chiefdom Capital.* University of Alabama Press, Tuscaloosa and London.

Kintigh, Keith W.
2000   Leadership Strategies in Protohistoric Zuni Towns. In *Alternative Leadership Strategies in the Prehispanic Southwest*, edited by Barbara J. Mills, pp. 95–116. University of Arizona Press, Tucson.

Knight, Vernon J., Jr.
1985   Theme and Variation in Mississippian Ritual Expression. In *Indians, Colonists, and Slaves: Essays in Memory of Charles H. Fairbanks*, edited by Kenneth W. Johnson, Jonathan M. Leader, and Robert C. Wilson, pp. 105–116. Special Publication Number 4, *Florida Journal of Anthropology*.
1989a   Some Speculations on Mississippian Monsters. In *The Southeastern Ceremonial Complex: Artifacts and Analysis*, edited by Patricia Galloway, pp. 206–210. University of Nebraska Press, Lincoln and London.
1989b   Symbolism of Mississippian Mounds. In *Powhatan's Mantle: Indians in the Colonial Southeast*, edited by Peter H. Wood, Gregory A. Waselkov, and M. Thomas Hatley, pp. 279–291. University of Nebraska Press, Lincoln and London.
1990   Social Organization and the Evolution of Hierarchy in Southeastern Chiefdoms. *Journal of Anthropological Research* 46(1):1–22.
1997   Some Developmental Parallels between Cahokia and Moundville. In *Cahokia: Domination and Ideology in the Mississippian World*, edited by Timothy R. Pauketat and Thomas E. Emerson, pp. 229–247. University of Nebraska Press, Lincoln and London.
1998   Moundville as a Diagrammatic Ceremonial Center. In *Archaeology of the Moundville Chiefdom*, edited by Vernon J. Knight, Jr., and Vincas P. Steponaitis, pp. 44–62. Smithsonian Institution Press, Washington and London.

2001   Feasting and the Emergence of Platform Mound Ceremonialism in Eastern
        North America. In *Feasts: Archaeological and Ethnographic Perspectives on Food,
        Politics, and Power,* edited by Michael Dietler and Brian Hayden, pp. 311–333.
        Smithsonian Institution Press, Washington, D.C.

2004   Characterizing Elite Midden Deposits at Moundville. *American Antiquity*
        69(2):304–321.

Knight, Vernon James, Jr., and Vincas P. Steponaitis

1998   A New History of Moundville. In *Archaeology of the Moundville Chiefdom,*
        edited by Vernon James Knight, Jr., and Vincas P. Steponaitis, pp. 1–25. Smith-
        sonian Institution Press, Washington, D.C.

Lacquement, Cameron H.

2004   How to Build a Mississippian House: A Study of Domestic Architecture in West-
        Central Alabama. Unpublished Master's thesis, Department of Anthropology,
        University of Alabama, Tuscaloosa.

Larson, Lewis H., Jr.

1957   An Unusual Wooden Rattle from the Etowah Site. *The Missouri Archaeologist*
        19(4):7–11.

1971   Archaeological Implications of Social Stratification at the Etowah Site, Georgia.
        In *Approaches to Social Dimensions of Mortuary Practices,* edited by James A.
        Brown, pp. 58–69. Memoir No. 25. Society for American Archaeology, Wash-
        ington, D.C.

1989   The Etowah Site. In *The Southeastern Ceremonial Complex: Artifacts and
        Analysis,* edited by Patricia Galloway, pp. 133–141. University of Nebraska
        Press, Lincoln.

1994   The Case for Earth Lodges in the Southeast. In *Ocmulgee Archaeology, 1936–
        1986,* edited by David J. Hally, pp. 105–115. University of Georgia Press,
        Athens.

Lefler, Hugh T. (editor)

1967   *A New Voyage to Carolina* by John Lawson. University of North Carolina Press,
[1709] Chapel Hill.

Lewis, R. Barry, and Charles Stout

1998   The Town as Metaphor. In *Mississippian Towns and Sacred Spaces: Searching for
        an Architectural Grammar,* edited by R. Barry Lewis and Charles Stout, pp. 227–
        241. University of Alabama Press, Tuscaloosa.

Lewis, R. Barry, Charles Stout, and Cameron B. Wesson

1998   The Design of Mississippian Towns. In *Mississippian Towns and Sacred Spaces:
        Searching for an Architectural Grammar,* edited by R. Barry Lewis and Charles
        Stout, pp. 1–21. University of Alabama Press, Tuscaloosa.

Lewis, Thomas M. N., and Madeline Kneberg

1970   *Hiwassee Island: An Archaeological Account of Four Tennessee Indian Peoples.* Re-
        printed. University of Tennessee Press, Knoxville. Originally published 1946,
        University of Tennessee Press.

Lewis, Thomas M. N., and Madeline D. Kneberg Lewis

1995   *The Prehistory of the Chickamauga Basin in Tennessee,* edited by Lynne P. Sulli-
        van. University of Tennessee Press, Knoxville.

Lindauer, Owen, and John H. Blitz

1997   Higher Ground: The Archaeology of North American Platform Mounds. *Journal
        of Archaeological Research* 5(2):169–207.

Lowry, Edward M.
 1939   Summary of the Excavations at the Frutchey Mound. Manuscript on file, Research Laboratories of Archaeology, University of North Carolina, Chapel Hill.
Lyon, Edwin A.
 1996   *A New Deal for Southeastern Archaeology.* University of Alabama Press, Tuscaloosa.
Marcus, Joyce, and Kent V. Flannery
 1996   *Zapotec Civilization: How Urban Society Evolved in Mexico's Oaxaca Valley.* Thames and Hudson, London.
Maxham, Mintcy D.
 2000   Rural Communities in the Black Warrior Valley, Alabama: The Role of Commoners in the Creation of the Moundville I Landscape. *American Antiquity* 65(2):337–354.
 2004   Native Constructions of Landscapes in the Black Warrior Valley, Alabama, A.D. 1020–1520. Unpublished Ph.D. dissertation, Department of Anthropology, University of North Carolina, Chapel Hill.
McGill, Robert, John W. Tukey, and Wayne A. Larsen
 1978   Variations of Box Plots. *The American Statistician* 32(1):12–16.
McGuire, Randall H., and Michael B. Schiffer
 1983   A Theory of Architectural Design. *Journal of Anthropological Archaeology* 2:277–303.
McWilliams, Richebourg Gaillard (translator and editor)
 1988   *Fleur de Lys and Calumet: Being the Pénicaut Narrative of French Adventure in Louisiana.* Originally published 1953. University of Alabama Press, Tuscaloosa.
Milanich, Jerald T., Ann S. Cordell, Vernon J. Knight, Jr., Timothy A. Kohler, and Brenda J. Sigler-Lavelle
 1997   *Archaeology of Northern Florida, A.D. 200–900: The McKeithen Weeden Island Culture.* Reprinted. University Press of Florida, Gainesville. Originally published 1984, Academic Press, Inc.
Milner, George R.
 1998   *The Cahokia Chiefdom: The Archaeology of a Mississippian Society.* Smithsonian Institution Press, Washington, D.C.
Milner, George R., and Sissel Schroeder
 1999   Mississippian Sociopolitical Systems. In *Great Towns and Regional Polities in the Prehistoric American Southwest and Southeast,* edited by Jill E. Neitzel, pp. 95–107. University of New Mexico Press, Albuquerque.
Mooney, James
 1890   The Cherokee Ball Play. *American Anthropologist* 3(2):105–132.
Moore, Alexander (editor)
 1988   *Nairne's Muskhogean Journals: The 1708 Expedition to the Mississippi River.* University Press of Mississippi, Jackson.
Mountjoy, Joseph B.
 1989   Early Radiocarbon Dates from a Site on the Pee Dee–Siouan Frontier in the Piedmont of Central North Carolina. *Southern Indian Studies* 38:7–21.
Muller, Jon
 1997   *Mississippian Political Economy.* Plenum Press, New York.
Oliver, Billy L.
 1992   Settlements of the Pee Dee Culture. Unpublished Ph.D. dissertation, Department of Anthropology, University of North Carolina, Chapel Hill.

O'Neill, Charles E. (editor)
  1977 *Charlevoix's Louisiana: Selections from the History and the Journal.* Louisiana
       State University Press, Baton Rouge.
Pauketat, Timothy R.
  1992 The Reign and Ruin of the Lords of Cahokia: A Dialectic of Dominance. In
       *Lords of the Southeast: Social Inequality and the Native Elites of Southeastern
       North America,* edited by Alex W. Barker and Timothy R. Pauketat, pp. 31–51.
       Archeological Paper Number 3. American Anthropological Association, Wash-
       ington, D.C.
  1993 *Temples for Cahokia Lords: Preston Holder's 1955–1956 Excavations of Kunne-
       mann Mound.* Memoir Number 26. Museum of Anthropology, University of
       Michigan, Ann Arbor.
  1994 *The Ascent of Chiefs: Cahokia and Mississippian Politics in Native North America.*
       University of Alabama Press, Tuscaloosa.
Pauketat, Timothy R., and Thomas E. Emerson
  1997 Introduction: Domination and Ideology in the Mississippian World. In *Cahokia:
       Domination and Ideology in the Mississippian World,* edited by Timothy R. Pauke-
       tat and Thomas E. Emerson, pp. 1–29. University of Nebraska Press, Lincoln.
Pauketat, Timothy R., Lucretia S. Kelly, Gayle J. Fritz, Neal H. Lopinot, Scott Elias, and
Eve Hargrave
  2002 Residues of Feasting and Public Ritual at Early Cahokia. *American Antiquity*
       67(2):257–279.
Payne, Claudine
  1994 Mississippian Capitals: An Archaeological Investigation of Precolumbian Po-
       litical Structure. Unpublished Ph.D. dissertation, Department of Anthropology,
       University of Florida, Gainesvelle.
Peebles, Christopher S.
  1971 Moundville and Surrounding Sites: Some Structural Considerations of Mortu-
       ary Practices II. In *Approaches to the Social Dimensions of Mortuary Practices,*
       edited by James A. Brown, pp. 68–91. Memoir Number 25. Society for American
       Archaeology, Washington, D.C.
Peebles, Christopher S., and Susan M. Kus
  1977 Some Archaeological Correlates of Ranked Societies. *American Antiquity*
       42(3):421–448.
Perdue, Theda
  1998 *Cherokee Women.* University of Nebraska Press, Lincoln.
Phillips, Philip, and James A. Brown
  1978 *Pre-Columbian Shell Engravings from the Craig Mound at Spiro, Oklahoma.*
       Peabody Museum Press, Cambridge, Massachusetts.
Polhemus, Richard R.
  1987 *The Toqua Site: A Late Mississippian Dallas Phase Town.* Report of Investigations
       Number 41. Department of Anthropology, University of Tennessee. Publica-
       tions in Anthropology 44. Tennessee Valley Authority, Knoxville.
  1990 Dallas Phase Architecture and Sociopolitical Structure. In *Lamar Archaeology:
       Mississippian Chiefdoms in the Deep South,* edited by Mark Williams and Gary
       Shapiro, pp. 125–138. University of Alabama Press, Tuscaloosa.
Reid, James J., Jr.
  1965 A Comparative Statement on Ceramics from the Hollywood and the Town
       Creek Mounds. *Southern Indian Studies* 17:12–25.

1967   Pee Dee Pottery from the Mound at Town Creek. Unpublished Master's thesis, Department of Anthropology, University of North Carolina, Chapel Hill.

1985   Formation Processes for the Practical Prehistorian: An Example from the Southeast. In *Structure and Process in Southeastern Archaeology,* edited by Roy S. Dickens, Jr., and H. Trawick Ward, pp. 11–33. University of Alabama Press, Tuscaloosa.

Rodning, Christopher B.

1999   Archaeological Perspectives on Gender and Women in Traditional Cherokee Society. *The Journal of Cherokee Studies* 10:3–27.

2001   Mortuary Ritual and Gender Ideology in Protohistoric Southwestern North Carolina. In *Archaeological Studies of Gender in the Southeastern United States,* edited by Jane M. Eastman and Christopher B. Rodning, pp. 77–100. University Press of Florida, Gainesville.

2002   The Townhouse at Coweeta Creek. In *Revisiting Coweeta Creek,* edited by Christopher B. Rodning and Amber M. VanDerwarker, special thematic section, *Southeastern Archaeology* 21(1):10–20.

2004   The Cherokee Town at Coweeta Creek. Unpublished Ph.D dissertation, Department of Anthropology, University of North Carolina, Chapel Hill.

Rodning, Christopher B., and Jane M. Eastman

2001   Gender and the Archaeology of the Southeast. In *Archaeological Studies of Gender in the Southeastern United States,* edited by Jane M. Eastman and Christopher B. Rodning, pp. 1–9. University Press of Florida, Gainesville.

Rudolph, James L.

1984   Earthlodges and Platform Mounds: Changing Public Architecture in the Southeastern U.S. *Southeastern Archaeology* 3(1):33–45.

Rudolph, James L. and David J. Hally

1985   *Archaeological Investigations at the Beaverdam Creek Site (9EB85), Elbert County, Georgia.* Department of Anthropology, University of Georgia. Submitted to United States Department of the Interior, Contract Number CX 5000-0-4043. National Park Service, Archaeological Services, Atlanta, Georgia.

Ryba, Elizabeth Anne

1997   Summit Architecture on Mound E at Moundville. Unpublished Master's thesis, Department of Anthropology, University of Alabama, Tuscaloosa.

Sattler, Richard A.

1995   Women's Status among the Muskogee and Cherokee. In *Women and Power in Native North America,* edited by Laura F. Klein and Lillian A. Ackerman, pp. 214–229. University of Oklahoma Press, Norman.

Saxe, Arthur A.

1970   Social Dimensions of Mortuary Practices. Unpublished Ph.D. dissertation, Department of Anthropology, University of Michigan, Ann Arbor.

1971   Social Dimensions of Mortuary Practices in a Mesolithic Population from Wadi Halfa, Sudan. In *Approaches to the Social Dimensions of Mortuary Practices,* edited by James A. Brown, pp. 39–57. Number 25. Memoirs of the Society for American Archaeology, Washington, D.C.

Scarry, John F.

1992   Political Offices and Political Structure: Ethnohistoric and Archaeological Perspectives on the Native Lords of Apalachee. In *Lords of the Southeast: Social In-*

equality and the Native Elites of Southeastern North America, edited by Alex W.
Barker and Timothy R. Pauketat, pp. 163–179. Archeological Paper Number 3.
American Anthropological Association, Washington, D.C.

1996   The Nature of Mississippian Societies. In *Political Structure and Change in the Prehistoric Southeastern United States,* edited by John F. Scarry, pp. 12–24. University Press of Florida, Gainesville.

Schiffer, Michael B.

1987   *Formation Processes of the Archaeological Record.* University of New Mexico Press, Albuquerque.

Schnell, Frank T., Vernon J. Knight, Jr., and Gail S. Schnell

1981   *Cemochechobee: Archaeology of a Mississippian Ceremonial Center on the Chatta-hoochee River.* University Presses of Florida, Gainesville.

Schroedl, Gerald F.

1986   Structures. In *Overhill Cherokee Archaeology at Chota-Tanasee,* edited by Gerald F. Schroedl, pp. 217–272. Report of Investigations 38. Department of Anthropology, University of Tennessee. Publications in Anthropology 42. Tennessee Valley Authority, Knoxville.

1998   Mississippian Towns in the Eastern Tennessee Valley. In *Mississippian Towns and Sacred Spaces: Searching for an Architectural Grammar,* edited by R. Barry Lewis and Charles Stout, pp. 64–92. University of Alabama Press, Tuscaloosa.

Schroedl, Gerald F., and C. Clifford Boyd, Jr.

1991   Late Woodland Period Culture in East Tennessee. In *Stability, Transformation, and Variation: The Late Woodland Southeast,* edited by Michael S. Nassaney and Charles R. Cobb, pp. 69–90. Plenum Press, New York.

Shapiro, Gary

1984   Ceramic Vessels, Site Permanence, and Group Size: A Mississippian Example. *American Antiquity* 49(4):696–712.

Shapiro, Gary, and Bonnie G. McEwan

1992   Archaeology at San Luis Part One: The Apalachee Council House. *Florida Archaeology* 6:1–77.

Shennan, Stephen

1997   *Quantifying Archaeology.* University of Iowa Press, Iowa City.

Shepard, Anna O.

1957   *Ceramics for the Archaeologist.* Carnegie Institution of Washington, Washington, D.C.

Skibo, James M.

1992   *Pottery Function: A Use Alteration Perspective.* Plenum Press, New York.

Smith, Bruce D.

1978   Variation in Mississippian Settlement Patterns. In *Mississippian Settlement Patterns,* edited by Bruce D. Smith, pp. 479–503. Academic Press, New York.

1986   The Archaeology of the Southeastern United States: From Dalton to de Soto, 10,500–500 B.P. In *Advances in World Archaeology,* edited by Fred Wendorf and Angela E. Close, pp. 1–92. Academic Press, New York.

1992   Mississippian Elites and Solar Alignments—A Reflection of Managerial Necessity, or Levers of Social Inequality? In *Lords of the Southeast: Social Inequality and the Native Elites of Southeastern North America,* edited by Alex W. Barker and Timothy R. Pauketat. Archeological Paper Number 3. American Anthropological Association, Washington, D.C.

Smith, Marion F., Jr.
1988   Function from Whole Vessel Shape: A Method and an Application to Anasazi Black Mesa, Arizona. *American Anthropologist* 90:912–923.

Smith, Marvin T.
1994   *Archaeological Investigations at the Dyar Site, 9GE5.* Report Number 32. Laboratory of Archaeology Series, University of Georgia, Athens.

Smith, Marvin T., and Mark Williams
1994   Mississippian Mound Refuse Disposal Patterns and Implications for Archaeological Research. *Southeastern Archaeology* 13(1):27–35.

South, Stanley
1957a Town Creek Weekly Report. Manuscript on file, Research Laboratories of Archaeology, University of North Carolina, Chapel Hill.
1957b Untitled Map. Map on file, Research Laboratories of Archaeology, University of North Carolina, Chapel Hill.
2002   *Archaeological Pathways to Historic Site Development.* Kluwer Academic/Plenum Publishers, New York.

Speck, Frank G.
1979   *Ethnology of the Yuchi Indians.* Reprinted. Humanities Press, Atlantic Highlands, New Jersey. Originally published 1909, Anthropological Publications of the University Museum Volume 1, Number 1, University of Pennsylvania, Philadelphia.

Steponaitis, Vincas P.
1978   Location Theory and Complex Chiefdoms: A Mississippian Example. In *Mississippian Settlement Patterns,* edited by Bruce D. Smith, pp. 417–453. Academic Press, New York.
1986   Prehistoric Archaeology in the Southeastern United States, 1970–1985. *Annual Review of Anthropology* 15:363–404.
1998   Population Trends at Moundville. In *Archaeology of the Moundville Chiefdom,* edited by Vernon J. Knight, Jr., and Vincas P. Steponaitis, pp. 26–43. Smithsonian Institution Press, Washington, D.C.

Stuart, George E.
1975   The Post-Archaic Occupation of Central South Carolina. Unpublished Ph.D. dissertation, Department of Anthropology, University of North Carolina, Chapel Hill.

Stuiver, Minze, Paula J. Reimer, and Ron Reimer
2005   CALIB Radiocarbon Calibration. Electronic document, http://radiocarbon. pa.qub.ac.uk/calib, accessed March 18, 2005.

Sullivan, Lynne P.
1987   The Mouse Creek Phase Household. *Southeastern Archaeology* 6(1):16–29.
1995   Mississippian Household and Community Organization in Eastern Tennessee. In *Mississippian Communities and Households,* edited by J. Daniel Rogers and Bruce D. Smith, pp. 99–123. University of Alabama Press, Tuscaloosa.
2001   Those Men in the Mounds: Gender, Politics, and Mortuary Practices in Late Prehistoric Eastern Tennessee. In *Archaeological Studies of Gender in the Southeastern United States,* edited by Jane M. Eastman and Christopher B. Rodning, pp. 101–126. University Press of Florida, Gainesville.

Swanton, John R.
1911   *Indian Tribes of the Lower Mississippi Valley and Adjacent Coast of the Gulf of*

Mexico. Bulletin 43. Bureau of American Ethnology, Smithsonian Institution, Government Printing Office, Washington, D.C.

1979 *The Indians of the Southeastern United States.* Reprinted. Smithsonian Institution Press, Washington, D.C. Originally published 1946, Bulletin Number 137, Bureau of American Ethnology, United States Government Printing Office, Washington, D.C.

1993 *Source Material for the Social and Ceremonial Life of the Choctaw Indians.* Reprinted. Birmingham Public Library Press, Birmingham, Alabama. Originally published 1931, Bulletin Number 103, Bureau of American Ethnology, United States Government Printing Office, Washington, D.C.

1996 *Source Material on the History and Ethnology of the Caddo Indians.* Reprinted. University of Oklahoma Press, Norman. Originally published 1942, Bulletin Number 132, Bureau of American Ethnology, Smithsonian Institution, Washington, D.C.

Swart, John

1940a Mg°2 First Quarterly Report. Manuscript on file, Research Laboratories of Archaeology, University of North Carolina, Chapel Hill.

1940b Mg°2 Second Quarterly Report. Manuscript on file, Research Laboratories of Archaeology, University of North Carolina, Chapel Hill.

Taft, Kristi E.

1996 Functionally Relevant Classes of Pottery at Moundville. Unpublished Master's thesis, Department of Anthropology, University of Alabama, Tuscaloosa.

Thomas, Larissa

2001 The Gender Division of Labor in Mississippian Households. In *Archaeological Studies of Gender in the Southeastern United States,* edited by Jane M. Eastman and Christopher B. Rodning, pp. 27–56. University Press of Florida, Gainesville.

Trinkley, Michael B.

1980 Investigation of the Woodland Period along the South Carolina Coast. Unpublished Ph.D. dissertation, Department of Anthropology, University of North Carolina, Chapel Hill.

Turner, Christy G. II, and Laurel Lofgren

1966 Household Size of Prehistoric Western Pueblo Indians. *Southwestern Journal of Anthropology* 22:117–132.

VanDerwarker, Amber M.

1999 Feasting and Status at the Toqua Site. *Southeastern Archaeology* 18(1):24–34.

Ward, H. Trawick, and R. P. Stephen Davis, Jr.

1993 *Indian Communities on the North Carolina Piedmont, A.D. 1000 to 1700.* Monograph Number 2. Research Laboratories of Anthropology, University of North Carolina, Chapel Hill.

1999 *Time before History: The Archaeology of North Carolina.* University of North Carolina Press, Chapel Hill.

Waselkov, Gregory A.

1989 Seventeenth-Century Trade in the Colonial Southeast. *Southeastern Archaeology* 8(2):117–133.

Waselkov, Gregory A., and Kathryn E. Holland Braund (editors)

1995 *William Bartram on the Southeastern Indians.* University of Nebraska Press, Lincoln.

Wauchope, Robert
1966 *Archaeological Survey of Northern Georgia with a Test of Some Cultural Hypotheses.* Memoir Number 21. Society for American Archaeology, Salt Lake City.

Welch, Paul D.
1991 *Moundville's Economy.* University of Alabama Press, Tuscaloosa.

Welch, Paul D., and C. Margaret Scarry
1995 Status-Related Variation in Foodways in the Moundville Chiefdom. *American Antiquity* 60(3):397–419.

Wesson, Cameron B.
1998 Mississippian Sacred Landscapes: The View from Alabama. In *Mississippian Towns and Sacred Spaces: Searching for an Architectural Grammar,* edited by R. Barry Lewis and Charles Stout, pp. 93–122. University of Alabama Press, Tuscaloosa.

Whalen, Michael E., and Paul E. Minnis
2000 Leadership at Casas Grandes, Chihuahua, Mexico. In *Alternative Leadership Strategies in the Prehispanic Southwest,* edited by Barbara J. Mills, pp. 168–179. University of Arizona Press, Tucson.

Whallon, Robert D.
1969 Rim Diameter, Vessel Volume, and Economic Prehistory. *Michigan Academician* 11(2):89–98.

Wilk, Richard R., and Robert McC. Netting
1984 Households: Changing Forms and Functions. In *Households: Comparative and Historical Studies of the Domestic Group,* edited by Robert McC. Netting, Richard R. Wilk, and Eric J. Arnould. University of California Press, Berkeley.

Williams, Mark, and Gary Shapiro (editors)
1990 *Lamar Archaeology: Mississippian Chiefdoms in the Deep South.* University of Alabama Press, Tuscaloosa.

Williams, Samuel Cole (editor)
1930 *Adair's History of the American Indians.* Originally published London. Promon-
[1775] tory Press, New York.

Wilson, Gregory D.
2001 Crafting Control and the Control of Crafts: Rethinking the Moundville Greenstone Industry. *Southeastern Archaeology* 20(2):118–128.

Wilson, Gregory D., and Christopher B. Rodning
2002 Boiling, Baking, and Pottery Breaking: A Functional Analysis of Ceramic Vessels from Coweeta Creek. In *Revisiting Coweeta Creek,* edited by Christopher B. Rodning and Amber M. VanDerwarker, special thematic section, *Southeastern Archaeology* 21(1):29–35.

Winter, Marcus C.
1976 The Archeological Household Cluster in the Valley of Oaxaca. In *The Early Mesoamerican Village,* edited by Kent V. Flannery, pp. 25–31. Academic Press, New York.

Worth, John E.
1998 *The Timucuan Chiefdoms of Spanish Florida,* Volume 1, *Assimilation.* University Press of Florida, Gainesville.

Index